Qui

MW01109833

(DDC)®

Excel 5
for Windows™

Karl Schwartz/Joanne Schwartz

DDC *Publishing*
14 East 38 St New York, NY 10016

Microsoft®, MS-DOS®, Access®, Fox Pro® and Visual Basic® are registered trademarks of Microsoft Corporation. AutoSum™ and Windows™ are trademarks of Microsoft Corporation.

Apple® and Macintosh® are registered trademarks of Apple Computer, Inc.

dBase® is a registered trademark of Borland International, Inc. Paradox® is a registered trademark of Ansa Software, a Borland Company.

IBM® is a registered trademark of International Business Machines Corporation.

1-2-3® and Lotus® are registered trademarks of Lotus Development Corporation. cc:Mail™ is a trademark of cc:Mail Inc., a wholly owned subsidiary of Lotus Development Corporation.

Btrieve® is a registered trademark of Novell, Inc.

ORACLE® is a registered trademark of Oracle Corporation.

Portions of the Microsoft Excel Solver program code are copyright 1990, 1991 and 1992 by Frontline Systems, Inc. Portions are copyright 1989 by Optimal Methods, Inc.

Screen shot(s) reprinted with permission from Microsoft Corporation.

All registered trademarks, trademarks and service marks are the property of their respective companies.

INTRODUCTION

Our **DDC Quick Reference Guide** for **Microsoft® Excel 5** is designed to help you perform Excel spreadsheet operations without searching through a lengthy manual for instructions.

- **Step-by-step instructions** allow you to look up and perform Excel 5 actions easily using a mouse. We explain basic mouse operations on page iii ⌫ .

- To make the procedures easy to follow, the steps include the same **graphic symbols** appearing on your Excel 5 screen.

- **Topics are grouped together** so related information is easy to find. (*See Table of Contents, page iv.*)

- Read **Before You Begin,** page ii, for advice on how best to use this book.

We are sure this guide will make it easier for you to use Microsoft Excel 5.0 for Windows.

Karl Schwartz and Joanne Schwartz

Technical Editor: Mildred Macdonald Tassone
English Editor: Rebecca Fiala
Editor: Kathy Berkemeyer
Design and Layout: Karl Schwartz, Joanne Schwartz

Before You Begin

If You Have Never Used a Mouse:

Read **Basic Mouse Operations**, page iii, for information on how to click, double-click and drag items with a mouse. Then, play Solitaire to practice these essential skills.

If You Are New to Windows:

Read and practice the skills in the **Getting Started** section, page 2. It contains instructions for selecting menus and dialog box options, and shows you how to work with Windows elements.

If You Are New to Excel:

Read **The Excel Window**, page 2, to get acquainted with the basic parts of the Excel Version 5 application window. Then read and practice the skills described in these important topics:

- **Select Cells**, page 42
- **Select Sheets**, page 36
- **About Cells**, page 238
- **About Formulas**, page 238
- **Relative, Absolute and Mixed Cell References**, pages 238 and 239

Reference Guide Conventions

This book uses the following format conventions:

TEXT FORMAT	INDICATES
Bold and Large	Menu names and items on a menu: • Click . . . . **File, Open...**
Bold	A specific name as it appears in Excel: • Select . . . . ☐ **Case Sensitive**
Bold and Italic	An object, object name or a major action that does not specifically appear: • Select . . . . ***cell(s) to delete***

Basic Mouse Operations

By default, the left mouse button is the primary mouse button. You can change the primary button and other mouse controls from Windows Control Panel. (Refer to your Windows documentation for help on how to customize a mouse.)

To point to an item:

* Move . . . . *the mouse*
  until the pointer touches desired item.
  The pointer is a graphic that moves as you move the mouse.
  The shape of the pointer changes depending upon the object
  it is pointing to and the kinds of actions it can do.

To click an item:

1 Point . . . . *to item*

2 Quickly press and release . . . . *left mouse button*

To right-click an item:

1 Point . . . . *to item*

2 Quickly press and release . . . . *right mouse button*

To double-click an item:

1 Point . . . . *to item*

2 Press and release . . . . *left mouse button*
  twice in rapid succession.

To drag an item (drag and drop):

1 Point . . . . *to item*

2 Press *and hold* . . . . *left mouse button*
  while moving . . . . *mouse*
  The item moves as you move the mouse.

3 Release . . . . *mouse button*
  to drop item at the current location.

iv

Table of Contents

Getting Started

Toolbars

Continued ...

V

Table of Contents — Toolbars (continued)

Manage Workbooks

Continued ...

vi

Continued ...

vii

Table of Contents — Edit Cells (continued)

Formulas and Functions

Continued ...

Table of Contents (continued)

Name Cells and Formulas

Calculate

Continued ...

Table of Contents — Calculate (continued)

Pivot Tables

Sorting

Continued ...

X

Table of Contents (continued)

Lists

Outline

Formatting

Continued ...

xi

Table of Contents — Formatting (continued)

Continued ...

xii

Styles

Printing

Reports and Views

Continued ...

xiii

Table of Contents (continued)

Workspace Views

Protecting Workbook Data

Graphic Objects

Continued ...

xiv

Table of Contents — Graphic Objects (continued)

Charts

Continued ...

Table of Contents — Charts (continued)

Object Linking and Embedding

Continued ...

xvi

Table of Contents (continued)

Continued ...

Table of Contents (continued)

Annotate and Audit Worksheet

Appendix

Run Excel

To run Excel from Program Manager:
FROM GROUP WINDOW CONTAINING EXCEL

- Double-click . . . . Microsoft Excel

To run Excel from File Manager:
FROM DIRECTORY WINDOW CONTAINING EXCEL

- Double-click . . . . excel.exe

  OR

  Double-click desired . . . . **Excel data file**

Set Excel Run Options

FROM PROGRAM MANAGER GROUP WINDOW CONTAINING EXCEL

1 Click . . . . Microsoft Excel

2 Click . . . . **File, Properties...**

3 Type or edit text in . . . . **Command Line:** ▢
using the following examples as a model:
EXCEL filename *(to open a specific file).*
EXCEL /R filename *(to open a specific file as read only).*
EXCEL /E *(to suppress creation of BOOK1.XLS).*

To assign a shortcut key:

- Press keys (e.g. Ctrl+E) in . . . . . . **Shortcut Key:** ▢

To specify a default working directory:

- Type path in . . . . **Working Directory:** ▢
  NOTE: *If the Default File Location option is specified
  (page 34), it will override the working directory specified here.
  If using the RUN command from Program Manager's File menu,
  you can type EXCEL /P path to specify the default working directory.
  Substitute the underlined word with an actual path
  (e.g., C:\YOURDIR).*

4 Click . . . . OK

The Excel Window

Use illustration below and the terms that follow it to get acquainted with the basic parts of the Excel Version 5 application window.

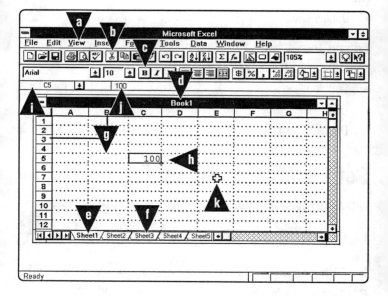

- The *Microsoft Excel application window* contains a **menu bar**[a] immediately below its title bar. You will use the menu bar to select commands the menu contains.

- Below the menu bar, Excel provides **buttons**[b,c] on two rows of **toolbars**[b,c] that you can use to select commands quickly, without opening a menu or dialog box.

- When you first run Excel 5, it opens a document window called a **workbook**[d] (Book1) that displays the active worksheet (Sheet1). Each workbook contains multiple worksheets (Sheet1, Sheet2 . . .) that you will use to enter your data and formulas.

Continued ...

The Excel Window (continued)

- **Sheet tabs**[f], at the bottom of the workbook window, provide an easy way for you to switch between worksheets. The **active worksheet tab**[e] is shown in bold (Sheet1).

- **Row and column headings**[g] in a worksheet form a grid of cells. You can use these headings to select an entire row or column of cells or to change the row or column size.

- Excel names each **cell**[h] by the intersection of it's row and column (cell reference). The **active cell**[h] contains a dark outline. When a cell is active, you can type data in it or edit the data the cell contains.

- Below the toolbars, Excel provides a **Name box**[i] — drop-down list showing the name, or cell reference, of the active cell. You can also use this list to go to a specific cell quickly.

- The **formula bar**[j] provides useful tools for typing or editing cell data.

- The **mouse pointer**[k] moves as you move the mouse. It's shape will change depending on what it can do in a given screen position. You can use the mouse pointer to select items such as cells, menu items, toolbar buttons, or worksheets.

Quit Excel

- Click .... **File, Exit**

  OR

  Press .... **Alt** + **F4**

  NOTE: *If you have not saved changes made to a workbook document, a message box, will appear prompting you to save them.*

Select Menu Items

The menus and menu items you see in the Excel application window will depend upon the situation or the current selection. For example, if no workbook is open, Excel will display only the File and Help menus. If an embedded chart or chart worksheet is selected, Excel will show menu items for charts.

If the menu or menu item you want is not available, do one of the following:

- *Select worksheet or worksheet item appropriate to action you want to take.*
- *Deselect object or cell.*
- *Click a cell to disable cell editing.*

To select a menu item from the menu bar:
The Excel window contains a menu bar just below the title bar.

1 Click . . . . **desired menu name**
   Excel will display a menu.

2 Click . . . . **desired menu item**

To open a shortcut menu and select an item:
Excel provides shortcut menus that pop-up when you right-click certain objects. The menu options apply to the object you clicked.

1 Right-click . . . . **object**
   Excel will display a menu.

2 Click . . . . **desired menu item**

To close a menu without selecting an item:

- Click . . . . **anywhere outside menu**

Example of menu items:

*A **check mark** (✓) indicates the item is already selected.*

*An **ellipsis** (...) indicates another window or dialog box will open when that item is selected.*

***Dimmed** commands are not appropriate to the current situation and cannot be selected.*

Continued ...

In this book, MENU steps will be shown as:

- Click .... **menu name, menu item**
  *where **menu name** is a name on the menu bar, and **menu item** is an*
  option on the open menu.

OR

- Click .... **menu name,** then select **menu item**
  *where **menu name** is a name on the menu bar, and **menu item** is an*
  option on the open menu whose setting can be selected (turned on) or
  deselected (turned off).

OR

1 Right-click .... ***object***
  *where **object** is a specified object.*

2 Click .... **menu item**
  *where **menu item** is an option on the shortcut menu.*

Dialog Box Elements

When Excel needs additional information to complete a command, a dialog box appears. Dialog boxes may contain the following elements:

- **Command buttons** carry out actions described in the button's name such as OK .

- A **check box** provides for the selection or deselection of an option. A selected check box ⊠ contains an X. More than one check box may be selected at a time in a group of check boxes.

- A **drop-down list box** provides a **drop-down list arrow** used to access a hidden list. Excel displays the currently selected list item in the box.

- An **increment box** provides a space for typing a value. Up and down arrows (usually to the right of the box) give you a way to select a value with the mouse.

- A **list box** displays a list of items from which selections can be made. A list box may have a scroll bar that can be used to show hidden items in the list.

- An **option button** ◯ provides for the selection of one option in a group of option buttons. A selected option button ⊙ contains a dark circle.

- A **scroll bar** is a horizontal or vertical bar providing scroll arrows and a scroll box that can be used to show hidden items in a list. (Also see **Scroll**, page 12.)

- A **text box** provides a space for typing in information.

- A **named tab**, such as Margins , provides a way to show options related to the tab's name in the same dialog box.

Select Options in a Dialog Box

To select an item in a DROP-DOWN LIST:

1 Click . . . . *list's drop-down arrow* ⊞

    If item is not in view,
- Click . . . . *scroll arrows* ⬆⬇
until item is in view.

2 Click . . . . *item*

In this book, DROP-DOWN LIST steps will be shown as:

> - Select item in . . . . **XYZ:** ⬚ ⊞
> *where XYZ is the name of the drop-down list.*

To select one item in a LIST BOX:

- Click . . . . *item*

    If item is not in view,
- **a** Click . . . . *scroll arrows* ⬆⬇
until item is in view.
- **b** Click . . . . *item*

To select consecutive items in a LIST BOX:

1 Click . . . . *first item*
2 Press Shift and click . . . . *last item in group*

To select multiple items in a LIST BOX:

- Press Ctrl while clicking . . . . *each item*

In this book, LIST BOX steps will be shown as:

> - Select item(s) in . . . . **XYZ** list
> *where XYZ is the name of the list box.*

Continued ...

8

Select Options in a Dialog Box (continued)

To type data in an empty TEXT BOX:

1 Click anywhere in . . . . *text box*

2 Type the data . . . . *data*

To replace data in a TEXT BOX:

1 Double-click . . . . *data to replace in text box* `data`
Existing data is highlighted.

2 Type . . . . *new data*

To edit data in a TEXT BOX:

1 Click . . . . *desired character position in text box* `data`

If editing is required,

- Press . . . . `Del`
  to remove characters to right of insertion point.
  OR
  Press . . . . `BkSp`
  to remove characters to left of insertion point.

2 Type . . . . *new data*

In this book, TEXT BOX steps will be shown as:

- Type information in . . . . **XYZ:**
  *where **XYZ** is the name of the text box.*

To select/deselect a CHECK BOX:

- Click . . . . ☐ *option name*
  to select (☒).
  OR
  Click . . . . ☒ *option name*
  to deselect (☐).

In this book, CHECK BOX steps will be shown as:

- Select or deselect . . . . ☐ **XYZ**
  *where **XYZ** is the name of the check box option.*

Continued ...

Select Options in a Dialog Box (continued)

To select an OPTION BUTTON:

NOTE: *Only one option button may be selected in a group.*

- Click . . . . ◯ *option name*
  to select (◉).

In this book, OPTION BUTTON steps will be shown as:

- Select . . . . ◯ **XYZ**
  *where **XYZ** is the name of the option.*

To select a COMMAND BUTTON:

- Click . . . . `command name`
  Selected command button carries out the command action.

In this book, COMMAND BUTTON steps will be shown as:

- Click . . . . `XYZ`
  *where **XYZ** is the name of the command button.*

To type or select a value in an INCREMENT BOX:

1 Click in . . . .

2 Type desired value . . . . *number*

OR

- Click . . . . *up or down increment arrows*
  The typed or selected value appears in the box.

In this book, INCREMENT BOX steps will be shown as:

- Type or select value in . . . . **XYZ:**
  *where **XYZ** is the name of the increment box.*

Continued ...

Select Options in a Dialog Box (continued)

To select a TAB in a dialog box:

- Click . . . .   XYZ

  *where **XYZ** is the name of the tab.*

In this book, SELECT TAB steps will be shown as:

- Click . . . .   XYZ

  *where **XYZ** is the name of the tab.*

Undo a Command

NOTE: *To successfully undo a command, undo before another command is selected.*
Not all commands can be undone.

- Click . . . . ***Undo button*** ↶

  OR

  Click . . . . **Edit, Undo**

Repeat a Command

NOTE: *To successfully repeat a command, repeat before another command is selected.*
Not all commands can be repeated.

- Click . . . . ***Repeat button*** ↷

  OR

  Click . . . . **Edit, Repeat**

Select Drive, Directory, or File(s)

FROM DIALOG BOX
NOTE: The dialog box options may vary depending on the command used.

To select a <u>drive</u>:

- Select desired drive letter in . . . . **Dri<u>v</u>es:** | ⯆ |

  Files in current directory of selected drive appear in File <u>N</u>ame list box.

To select a <u>directory</u>:

- Double-click directory name in . . . . **<u>D</u>irectories** list

  Files in selected directory appear in File <u>N</u>ame list box.

To list files of a different <u>type</u>:

- Select file type to list in . . . **List Files of <u>T</u>ype:** | ⯆ |

  Only files of specified type appear in File <u>N</u>ame list box.

  OR

  Type a new filespec in . . . . **File <u>N</u>ame:** | |

  Only files of specified type appear in File <u>N</u>ame list box.
  EXAMPLE: * .WK1 — *to list only files that have a WK1*
  filename extension.

To select file(s) in current directory:

- Select desired file in . . . . **File <u>N</u>ame** list

  OR

  Press **Ctrl** and click each file to select in . . . . . **File <u>N</u>ame** list

In this book, SELECT DRIVE, DIRECTORY, OR FILE(S) steps will be shown as:

- Select . . . . *drive* or *directory* or *file(s)*

Scroll
(Move an Area of Data into View)

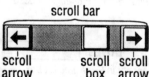

scroll bar
scroll arrow   scroll box   scroll arrow

One character left or right:

• Click . . . . *left or right scroll arrow*

One line up or down:

• Click . . . . *up or down scroll arrow*

To the beginning of a line or list:

• Drag . . . . *horizontal scroll box*
  to the extreme left of scroll bar.

To the end of a line or list:

• Drag . . . . *horizontal scroll box*
  to the extreme right of scroll bar.

To the beginning of a document or list:

• Drag . . . . *vertical scroll box*
  to the top of scroll bar.

To the end of a document or list:

• Drag . . . . *vertical scroll box*
  to the bottom of scroll bar.

One screen up or down:

• Click . . . . *vertical scroll bar*
  above or below scroll box.

One screen right or left:

• Click . . . . *horizontal scroll bar*
  to right or left of scroll box.

Window Elements

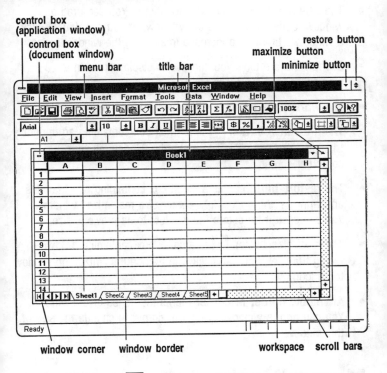

- The **control box** ⊟ provides access to a menu containing commands to help you control the window.

- **Application and document windows** represent the two basic kinds of windows in the Windows environment. Application windows have a larger control box symbol and also contain a menu bar. Document windows have a smaller control box symbol and are confined to the borders of the application to which they belong. Excel document windows are called workbooks.

- The **menu bar** is the list of menu names appearing immediately below the title bar in an application window.

Continued ...

Window Elements (continued)

- The **title bar** displays the window name. You can drag a window's title bar to move the window, or you can double-click a window's title bar to increase (maximize) the window's size.

- **Scroll bars** are tools you can use to display areas in a workspace that are not in view.

- The **workspace** is the area in a window where data is held.

- The **maximize button** ▲ is a small box containing an upright triangle. You can click it to make the window fill your computer screen.

- The **restore button** ⬍ is a small box containing two triangles appearing on the upper-right corner of a maximized window. You can click it to restore the window to its previous size.

- The **minimize button** ▼ is a small box containing a down-facing triangle. You can click it to reduce (minimize) the window to an icon.

- A **window border or corner** marks the edges of the window. You can drag a windows border or corner to change the size of the window.

Move a Window

- Drag . . . . *window's title bar to new location*

Move an Icon

- Drag . . . . *icon to new location*

Change Size of a Window

NOTE: *A maximized window must be restored (page 16) before it can be sized.*

1 Point . . . . **to border or corner of window to size**
  Pointer becomes one of the following: ⬁ ⬍ ⬌ ⬂ .

2 Drag . . . . **window outline to desired size**

3 Repeat steps until desired size is obtained.
  NOTE: *If the windows border can not be reached, you can use the keyboard to size the application or document window, as shown.*

  Application window . . . [Alt] + [Space] , [S] , [↕] (once), then [↕]
  Document window . . . . . . [Alt] + [▬] , [S] , [↕] (once), then [↕]

Minimize a Window

When you minimize an application window, it's reduced to an icon and placed on the bottom of the desktop (the area below all windows). Minimized document windows are reduced to icons and placed within their application's borders.

• Click . . . . **window's minimize button** [▾]
  NOTE: *A maximized document window will not have a minimize button. To minimize window, use steps* **1** *and* **2** *below.*

OR

1 Click . . . . **window's control box** [▭]
  NOTE: *The control box of a maximized document window is located on the left side of its application window's menu bar.*

2 Click . . . . **Minimize**

Maximize a Window

Application windows will expand to full-screen size.
Document windows will expand to the limit of their application's window borders, but will not extend over their application's title and menu bars.

To maximize window using its <u>maximize button</u>:

- Click . . . . *window's maximize button* 🔼
  NOTE: *After a window is maximized, the maximize button is replaced with a restore button.*

To maximize window using its <u>control box</u>:

1 Click . . . . *window's control box* ➖
2 Click . . . . **Ma_ximize**
  NOTE: *After a window is maximized, the maximize button is replaced with a restore button.*

To maximize window using its <u>title bar</u>:

- Double-click . . . . *window's* ▐ Title bar ▌
  NOTE: *After a window is maximized, the maximize button is replaced with a restore button.*

Restore a Maximized Window

NOTE: *The restore button of a maximized application window is located at the top right corner of its window.*
The restore button of a maximized document window is located on the right side of its application's menu bar.

FROM A MAXIMIZED WINDOW

- Click . . . . *maximized window's restore button* 🔽
  NOTE: *After a window is restored, the restore button is replaced with a maximize button.*

Show Purpose of any Toolbar Button

• Point to and rest pointer on .... *desired button*

Toolbar Shortcut Menu

1 Right-click .... *blank area on toolbar*

2 Select .... *desired menu option:*
Common toolbars (Standard, Formatting, Chart, Drawing,
Forms, Visual Basic, Auditing, WorkGroup, Microsoft),
Toolbar..., Customize...

Show or Hide a Toolbar

1 Click .... **View, Toolbars...**
*(Also see **Toolbar Shortcut Menu**, above.)*

2 Select or deselect desired toolbar(s) in .... **Toolbars** list
Toolbars list items include: *Standard, Formatting, Query and Pivot,*
Chart, Drawing, TipWizard, Forms, Stop Recording, Visual Basic,
Auditing, WorkGroup, Microsoft, Full Screen

3 Click .... OK

Move a Toolbar

You can dock a toolbar (between the menu bar and the formula bar or on the
edges of the Excel window), or have it float as a separate window. Toolbars
containing a drop-down list (i.e., the Formatting toolbar) cannot be docked on
the left or right edge of the Excel window.

1 Point to .... *blank area on toolbar*

   OR

   Point to .... *title bar of floating toolbar*

2 Drag .... *toolbar outline*
   onto .... *desired workspace position* or
                              desired docking position

   NOTE: *Excel shifts existing toolbars when you move a toolbar into*
   a docking position.

Switch between a Floating or Docking Toolbar

• Double-click . . . . *blank area on toolbar*

Size a Floating Toolbar

*(See **Change Size of a Window**, page 15.)*

Set General Toolbar Options

1 Click . . . . **View, Toolbars...**
*(Also see **Toolbar Shortcut Menu**, page 17.)*

2 Select or deselect . . . . **Toolbar options:**
Color Toolbars, Large Buttons, Show ToolTips

3 Click . . . . `OK`

Create a Customized Toolbar

1 Click . . . . **View, Toolbars...**
*(Also see **Toolbar Shortcut Menu**, page 17.)*

2 Type a unique toolbar name in . . . . **Toolbar Name:** [   ]

3 Click . . . . `New`
Excel displays an empty toolbar and opens the Customize dialog box.

To add a button to the new toolbar:

a Select a category in . . . . **Categories** list

   #### To see a button's description:

   1. Click desired button in . . . . **Buttons** box

   2. Read description at bottom of dialog box.

b Drag . . . . *desired button*
   onto . . . . *new toolbar*

c Repeat steps **a** and **b**, as needed.

4 Click . . . . `Close`

Save a Toolbar Configuration for Use in Other Work Sessions

Saves the current toolbar configuration (the arrangement of built-in and created toolbars) in a named file so you can bring it back at any time.

1 Configure .... ***toolbars***
2 Quit .... ***Excel***
3 Open .... ***File Manager***
4 Select .... ***directory containing Windows***
5 Copy and rename the .... ***EXCEL5.XLB file***

   NOTE: *Copy the file to your Excel directory, and give the copied file a name describing the toolbar configuration (such as MYCHART.XLB).*

Open a Saved Toolbar Configuration

Restores a toolbar layout saved (copied) to a named toolbar configuration file. (See above.)

1 Click .... **File, Open...**
2 Select filename of toolbar configuration in .... **File Name** list
3 Click .... OK

Attach Custom Toolbars to a Workbook

Ensures that a toolbar you have created will always be available from a specific workbook.

1 Click .... **Insert, Macro ▸, Module**
   OR
   Select .... *existing module sheet*
2 Click .... **Tools, Attach Toolbars...**
3 Select toolbar to attach in .... **Custom Toolbars** list
4 Click .... Copy >>
5 Repeat steps 3 and 4, as needed.
6 Click .... OK

Delete a Customized Toolbar

1 Click . . . . **View, Toolbars...**
(Also see Toolbar Shortcut Menu, page 17.)

2 Select toolbar to delete in . . . . **Toolbars** list

3 Click . . . . `Delete`

4 Click . . . . `OK`
to confirm deletion.

5 Click . . . . `OK`

Restore a Built-in Toolbar

1 Click . . . . **View, Toolbars...**
(Also see Toolbar Shortcut Menu, page 17.)

2 Select built-in toolbar to restore in . . . . **Toolbars** list

3 Click . . . . `Reset`
NOTE: If you do not see the reset button, you have selected a customized toolbar, not a built-in toolbar. Customized toolbars cannot be reset.

4 Click . . . . `OK`

Change Width of a Toolbar's Drop-down List

1 Right-click . . . . *blank area on toolbar*

2 Click . . . . **Customize...**

3 Click . . . . *border of* [⬙]
on toolbar in Excel window to change.
Excel surrounds drop-down list box with a thick border.

4 Point to . . . . *left or right border*
of drop-down list box to size.
Pointer becomes a ↔ when positioned correctly.

5 Drag . . . . *box outline left or right*

6 Click . . . . `Close`

Move a Toolbar Button

Groups a button with other buttons, adds space between buttons, moves a button to a new position on a toolbar, and moves a button to another toolbar. If you are moving a button to another tool bar, both toolbars must be in view.

1 Right-click . . . . **blank area on toolbar**

2 Click . . . . **Customize...**

3 Drag . . . . **button outline**
    to desired location on current or other toolbar.

4 Click . . . . | Close |

Copy a Toolbar Button

NOTE: *If you are copying a button to another tool bar, both toolbars must be in view.*

1 Right-click . . . . **blank area on toolbar**

2 Click . . . . **Customize...**

3 Press **Ctrl** and drag . . . . **button outline**
    to desired location on current or other toolbar.

4 Click . . . . | Close |

Use TipWizard

To turn TipWizard on or off:

- Click . . . . *TipWizard button*
  When on, Excel displays tips in the TipWizard box above the formula bar and any toolbar buttons it suggests to the right of the box.

To view other tips for the current work session:

- Click . . . .
  to the right of the TipWizard box.

Add or Remove Toolbar Buttons

1 Right-click . . . . *blank area on toolbar*
2 Click . . . . **Customize...**

To add a button:

   a Select category in . . . . **Categories** list

   To see a button's description:

      1. Click desired button in . . . . **Buttons** box

      2. Read description at bottom of dialog box.

   b Drag . . . . *desired button*
     to . . . . *desired position on toolbar*

   c Repeat steps **a** and **b**, as needed.

To remove a button:

   • Drag . . . . *button off toolbar*
3 Click . . . . `Close`

Copy Image of a Toolbar Button to Another Button

NOTE: Both the source and destination buttons must be in view.

1 Right-click . . . . *blank area on toolbar*
2 Click . . . . **Customize...**
3 Click . . . . *source button on toolbar*
4 Click . . . . **Edit, Copy Button Image**
5 Click . . . . *destination button on toolbar*
6 Click . . . . **Edit, Paste Button Image**
7 Click . . . . `Close`

Change Image of a Toolbar Button

NOTE: *You can copy an image (bitmap or picture) from another application onto the Clipboard, and then paste the image to the button. Follow steps 1-3 below, then click Paste Button Image from the shortcut menu.*

1 Right-click . . . . *blank area on toolbar*

2 Click . . . . **Customize...**

3 Right-click . . . . *button on toolbar to change*

4 Click . . . . **Edit Button Image...**

To erase entire image:

- Click . . . . `Clear`

To change or add colors:

a Select a color in . . . . **Colors** box

b Click or drag through . . . . *each pixel to color* in Picture box.

c Repeat steps **a** and **b**, as desired.

To move image:

- Click . . . . *arrow button* in direction to move image.

5 Click . . . . `OK`

Restore Image of a Toolbar Button

1 Right-click . . . . *blank area on toolbar*

2 Click . . . . **Customize...**

3 Right-click . . . . *button on toolbar to restore*

4 Click . . . . **Reset Button Image**

5 Click . . . . `Close`

Create a New Workbook

To open a new workbook based on the default template:

- Click . . . . *New Workbook button* 🗋
  on Standard toolbar.

To open a new workbook based on a saved template:

1 Click . . . . **File, New**
2 Select desired template in . . . . **New** list
3 Click . . . . `OK`

Open Recently Opened Workbook

By default, Excel lists the last four workbooks you worked with near the bottom of the File menu.

- Click . . . . **File,** *desired workbook name*

Open Duplicate Workbook Window

1 Select . . . . *workbook window to duplicate*
2 Click . . . . **Window, New Window**

Select a Workbook Window or Icon

- Click . . . . . . *workbook window* or *workbook icon* 📄

  OR

  Click . . . . **Window,** *name of workbook*
  near bottom of menu.

Open Existing Workbook

You can use this procedure to:
- *Open an existing workbook or workspace.*
- *Import a file from another application.*
- *Open a copy of a template file.*
- *Open more than one workbook at a time.*

1 Click . . . . *Open button* 🖼

on Standard toolbar.

OR

Click . . . . **File, Open...**

To list specific file formats for importing:

- Select a file type in . . . **List Files of Type:** [⬧]

To open file as read-only:

- Select . . . . ☐ **Read Only**

2 Select (page 11) . . . . *file(s) to open*

NOTES: *You can select multiple files by holding Ctrl while clicking each file you want to open in File Name list. If you open a template file, Excel will open a copy of the file and add a number to the end of its workbook name.*

3 Click . . . . [OK]

Open Original Template File

1 Click . . . . *Open button* 🖼

on Standard toolbar.

2 Select (page 11) . . . . *template file to open*

3 Press Shift and click . . . . [OK]

Arrange Workbook Windows

1 Click . . . . <u>W</u>indow, <u>A</u>rrange...

2 Select . . . . *Arrange option:*
<u>T</u>iled, H<u>o</u>rizontal, <u>V</u>ertical, <u>C</u>ascade

To arrange the active workbook's windows only:

• Select . . . . ☐ <u>W</u>indows of Active Workbook

3 Click . . . . [OK]

*NOTE: You can also arrange windows by moving them.
(See Move a Window, page 14).*

Arrange Workbook Icons

1 Click . . . . *any workbook icon* 📖

NOTE: Ignore display of the icon's control menu.

2 Click . . . . <u>W</u>indow, <u>A</u>rrange Icons
Excel arranges workbook icons on the bottom of the workspace.

Hide a Workbook

Hides a workbook from view, but does not close it.

1 Select . . . . *workbook to hide*

2 Click . . . . <u>W</u>indow, <u>H</u>ide

Unhide a Workbook

1 Click . . . . <u>W</u>indow, <u>U</u>nhide...

2 Select workbook to unhide in . . . . <u>U</u>nhide Workbook list

3 Click . . . . [OK]

Find Workbook Files (When a Search Criteria Has Been Previously Set)

You can use this procedure to:
- *Obtain a list of files based on a specified criteria.*
- *Preview workbook files in various ways.*
- *Manage workbook files (open, open as read-only, delete, copy, print, and sort).*
- *Create new directories for workbooks.*

1 Click . . . . **File, Find File...**

2 Select desired file in . . . . **Listed Files** list
*NOTE: To select multiple files, press **Ctrl** and click each file you want to select.*

To change view of selected file:

- Select desired view in . . . . **View** [⬦]
  View options include: Preview, File Info, Summary
  NOTE: Password protected workbooks cannot be previewed and their summary information cannot be viewed.

To issue a command on selected file:

a Click . . . . [Commands ▾]

b Select . . . . *command option:*
  Open Read Only, Print..., Summary..., Delete, Copy... (select to create directory), Sorting...

To sort file list:

a Click . . . . [Commands ▾]

b Select . . . . **Sorting...**

c Select . . . . **Sort Files By option:**
  Author, Creation Date, Last Saved By, Last Saved Date, Name, Size

d Select . . . . **List Files By option:**
  File Name, Title

e Click . . . . [OK]

Continued ...

Find Workbook Files — When a Search Criteria Has Been Previously Set (continued)

To set up a new search criteria:

a Click . . . . `Search...`

b Select (see below) . . . . *Search options*

To open selected file:

● Click . . . . `Open`

To close the Find File window:

● Click . . . . `Close`

Set Search Criteria (To Find Workbook Files)

1 Click . . . . **File, Find File...**

If Find File dialog box appears,

click . . . . `Search...`

NOTE: If a search criteria has been set up, the Find File dialog box will appear, showing the files matching the previously set criteria.

OR

FROM OPEN DIALOG BOX

a Click . . . . `Find File...`

b Click . . . . `Search...`

To select a saved search criteria:

● Select a search name in . . . . **Saved Searches** `▣`

To specify file or file type to search for:

● Type or select file or filespec in . . **File Name:** `▣`
NOTE: You can separate multiple filenames and filespecs with a semicolon (;).

To specify location to search:

● Type or select drive or directory in . . **Location:** `▣`

Continued ...

Set Search Criteria — To Find Workbook Files (continued)

To include subdirectories in search:

- Select . . . . ☐ **Include Subdirectories**

To rebuild file list of Listed Files:

- Select . . . . ☐ **Rebuild File List**

To set up an advanced search:

a Click . . . . [Advanced Search...]

To set location criteria:

1. Click . . . . [Location]

2. Fill in . . . . *desired location information*

To set summary criteria:

1. Click . . . . [Summary]

2. Fill in . . . . *desired summary information*
*NOTE: You can substitute wildcard characters (? *)
to represent any characters in a summary field.
You can also use the following search operators
(between the items you type) to narrow the criteria
for a search:*

    , *(comma)*   *match any item*
    & *(ampersand) or space* *match all items*
    ~ *(tilde)*   *does not match next item*
*To find data containing wildcards or the search operators,
you must enclose these special characters in quotation marks.*

To set time criteria:

1. Click . . . . [Timestamp]

2. Fill in . . . . *desired timestamp information*

b Click . . . . [OK]

To clear the current search criteria:

- Click . . . . [Clear]

Continued ...

30

Manage Workbooks

Set Search Criteria — To Find Workbook Files (continued)

To save search criteria:

a Click . . . . `Save Search As...`

b Type a unique name in . . . . . . **Search Name:** `[        ]`

c Click . . . . `OK`

To delete a saved search criteria:

a Select search name
to delete in . . . . **Saved Searches** `[     ▼]`

b Click . . . . `Delete Search...`

2 Click . . . . `OK`

3 Select (page 27) . . . . ***Find File options***

Close Active Workbook Window

*NOTE: If the window you are closing is the only window in the workbook,
the workbook also closes.*

• Click . . . . **File, Close**

OR

Double-click . . . . ***workbook's control-box*** `▭`
*NOTE: If you have not saved changes made to the workbook,
Excel will prompt you to save them.*

Close All Workbooks

1 Press **Shift** and click . . . . **File**

2 Click . . . . **Close All**
*NOTE: If you have not saved changes made to the workbooks,
Excel will prompt you to save them.*

Save Previously Saved Active Workbook

- Click . . . . *Save File button* 🔲
  on Standard toolbar.

  OR

  Click . . . . **File, Save**

  If Save As dialog box appears,
  NOTE: The Save As dialog box will appear if you have not previously saved the file, or if you opened the file as read-only.

  a If desired, select (page 11) . . . . *drive* or *directory*

  b Type filename in . . . . **File Name:** ▢

  c Click . . . . [OK]

Save Active Workbook As

*Saves and names the active workbook. (Also see **Save Active Workbook As (Options)**, page 32.)*

1 Click . . . . **File, Save As...**

2 If desired, select (page 11) . . . . *drive* or *directory*
   in which file will be saved.

3 Type filename in . . . . **File Name:** ▢

4 Click . . . . [OK]

Save Workspace

Saves the current arrangement of all open workbooks.

1 Click . . . . **File, Save Workspace...**

2 If desired, select (page 11) . . . . *drive* or *directory*
   in which workspace file will be saved.

3 Type filename in . . . . **File Name:** ▢

4 Click . . . . [OK]
   Excel will prompt you to save changes made to each open workbook.

Save Active Workbook As (Options)

You can use this procedure to:
- *Save a file in another format (export).*
- *Save a workbook as a template.*
- *Save and set save options (backup previous version, protection password, write reservation password, read-only recommendation).*

1 Click . . . . **File, Save As...**

2 If desired, select (page 11) . . . . **drive** or **directory** in which file will be saved.

   NOTE: If you are saving file as a template, select the EXCEL\XLSTART directory, so the template will appear when you open a new workbook.

3 Type filename in . . . . **File Name:** [   ]

To save file in a different format:

Exports files or saves them as templates.

- Select file format in . . . . . **Save File as Type:** [±]

To set save options for file:

a Click . . . . [Options...]

   ### To create a backup of previous version when saving:

   - Select . . . . ☐ **Always Create Backup**

   ### To password protect workbook:

   - Type password in . . . **Protection Password:** [   ]

   ### To prevent unauthorized users from saving workbook:

   - Type password in . . . . **Write Reservation Password:** [   ]

   ### To recommend document be opened as read-only:

   - Select . . . . ☐ **Read-Only Recommended**

b Click . . . . [OK]

c If prompted, reenter password(s).

4 Click . . . . [OK]

AutoSave Workbooks

Sets automatic saving of open workbooks.

1 Click . . . . **Tools, AutoSave...**
    NOTE: *If AutoSave does not appear on the Tools menu,*
    see **Install or Remove an Add-In**, *page 173.*

To enable/disable AutoSave:
- Select or deselect . . . . ☐ **Automatic Save Every**

To set time interval for AutoSave:
- Type number of minutes in . . . . [   ] **Minutes**

To automatically save active workbook only:
- Select . . . . ○ **Save Active Workbook Only**

To automatically save all open workbooks:
- Select . . . . ○ **Save All Open Workbooks**

To enable/disable prompt before automatic save:
- Select or deselect . . . . ☐ **Prompt Before Saving**

2 Click . . . . **OK**

View or Edit Active Workbook Summary

1 Click . . . . **File, Summary Info...**
2 Fill in . . . . *summary information:*
    Title (descriptive name of file), Subject (description of workbook),
    Author (Excel inserts name specified in User Name text box in
    Set General Workbook Options, *page 35), Keywords, Comments*

3 Click . . . . **OK**

Set General Workbook Options

Sets default workbook options, such as the standard font and number of sheets in a workbook.

1 Click .... **Tools, Options...**

2 Click .... | General |

To set reference style:

- Select .... ***Reference Style option:***
  A1 (default), R1C1 (columns and rows are labeled with numbers)

To set menu options:

- Select or deselect .... ***Menu options:***
  Recently Used File List, Microsoft Excel 4.0 Menus

To set Excel to ignore DDE requests:

- Select .... ☐ **Ignore Other Applications**

To set Excel to prompt for summary info when saving a new workbook:

- Select .... ☐ **Prompt for Summary Info**

To reset TipWizard:

- Select .... ☐ **Reset TipWizard**

To specify number of sheets in new workbook:

- Type or select
  number in .... **Sheets in New Workbook:** | ⇕ |

To set standard font:

- Select font in .... **Standard Font:** | Arial ▼ |

To set standard font size:

- Type or select font size in .... **Size:** | 10 ▼ |

To set default file location:

- Type path in .... **Default File Location:** | |

Continued ...

Set General Workbook Options (continued)

To specify an alternate startup location:

*Sets an additional directory location (in addition to XLSTART)
where you can store files that will open automatically, or
templates that will be available in the New dialog box.*

• Type path in . . **Alternate Startup File Location:** [　　　]

To specify user name:

*Adds the name you specify to file sharing, summary information,
scenario, and view dialogs the next time you start Excel.*

• Type name in . . . . **User Name:** [　　　]

3   Click . . . . [OK]

Manage Sheets in Workbooks

*By default, new workbooks contain worksheets labeled Sheet1, Sheet2 etc.
You can delete, rename, move, copy, and hide sheets. You can also insert
sheets of the following types: Worksheet, Chart, MS Excel 4.0 Macro,
Module, and Dialog.*

Workbook name

	A	B	C	D	E	
Book1						
1						
2						
3						
4						
5						
6						
7						
8						
9						
10						
11						
12						
13					*scroll bars*	
14						
15						

Sheet1 / Sheet2 / Sheet3

tab scrolling buttons   *active sheet tab*   *tab/scroll split bar*

Select Sheets

Selects the following sheet types: Worksheet, Chart, MS Excel 4.0 Macro, Module, and Dialog.

NOTE: *You select sheets by selecting their sheet tabs, located on the bottom of the workbook window. Selected sheet tabs are white, the active sheet tab is bold. Use the tab scrolling buttons (illustrated below) to view hidden sheet tabs. If no sheets are visible, see **Set View Options**, page 173.*

*scroll sheet tabs
left/right*

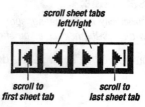

*scroll to
first sheet tab*

*scroll to
last sheet tab*

To select <u>one</u> sheet:

1 If necessary, click . . . . . *tab scrolling buttons* |◀ ◀ ▶ ▶|
to scroll a hidden sheet tab into view.

2 Click . . . . `\ Sheet # /`
where *Sheet #* is the name of the sheet to select.

To select <u>all</u> sheets:

1 Right-click . . . . `\ Sheet # /`
where *Sheet #* is the name of any sheet.

2 Click . . . . **Select All Sheets**

To select (group) <u>consecutive</u> sheets:

IMPORTANT: *When you group worksheets, entries and formatting applied to one worksheet are duplicated on all worksheets in the group.*

1 If necessary, click . . . . . *tab scrolling buttons* |◀ ◀ ▶ ▶|
to scroll hidden sheet tabs into view.

2 Click . . . . `\ Sheet # /`
where *Sheet #* is the name of the first sheet to select.

3 Press **Shift** and click . . . . `\ Sheet # /`
where *Sheet #* is the name of the last sheet in group to select.
[Group] appears in title bar.

Continued ...

Select Sheets (continued)

To select (group) <u>non-consecutive</u> sheets:
IMPORTANT: When you group worksheets, entries and formatting applied to one worksheet are duplicated on all worksheets in the group.

1 If necessary, click ..... *tab scrolling buttons* ⟦◄◄ ▶▶⟧
to scroll hidden sheet tabs into view.

2 Click .... ⟍ Sheet # ⟋
where *Sheet #* is the name of the first sheet to select.

3 Press **Ctrl** and click each .... ⟍ Sheet # ⟋
where *Sheet #* is the name of each sheet to select.
[Group] appears in title bar.

Deselect Grouped Sheets

• Click .... ⟍ Sheet # ⟋
where *Sheet #* is the name of any sheet that is not in group.

OR

1 Right-click .... ⟍ Sheet # ⟋
where *Sheet #* is the name of a sheet in group.

2 Click .... **Ungroup Sheets**

Hide a Sheet

NOTE: If a workbook has only one sheet, the sheet can not be hidden.

1 Select .... *sheet to hide*

2 Click .... **Format, Sheet** ▶

3 Click .... **Hide**

Unhide a Sheet

1 Click .... **Format, Sheet** ▸
2 Click .... **Unhide..**
3 Select sheet to unhide in .... **Unhide Sheet** list
4 Click .... ☐ OK ☐

Insert Sheets

To insert one sheet:
1 Right-click .... ＼Sheet #／
where *Sheet #* is the name of sheet before which
new sheet will be inserted.

2 Click .... **Insert...**
3 Select type of sheet to insert in .... **New** list
If chart was selected,
• Follow the ChartWizard (page 187) prompts.

4 Click .... ☐ OK ☐
Excel inserts sheet and makes the new sheet active.

To insert multiple worksheets:
1 Select .... *consecutive number of sheets to insert*
2 Right-click .... ＼Sheet #／
where *Sheet #* is the name of sheet before which new sheets
will be inserted.

3 Click .... **Insert...**
4 Select **Worksheet** in .... **New** list
5 Click .... ☐ OK ☐
Excel inserts sheets and makes the first new sheet active.

Delete Sheets

To delete <u>one</u> sheet:

1 Right-click . . . . ⟍ Sheet # ⟋
   where *Sheet #* is the name of sheet to delete.

2 Click . . . . **Delete**

3 Click . . . . ☐ OK ☐

To delete <u>multiple</u> sheets:

1 Select . . . . *sheets to delete*

2 Right-click . . . . ⟍ Sheet # ⟋
   where *Sheet #* is the name of a selected sheet.

3 Click . . . . **Delete**

4 Click . . . . ☐ OK ☐

Rename a Sheet

1 Double-click . . . . ⟍ Sheet # ⟋
   where *Sheet #* is the name of sheet to rename.

   OR

   a Right-click . . . . ⟍ Sheet # ⟋
      where *Sheet #* is the name of sheet to rename.

   b Click . . . . **Rename...**

2 Type new name in . . . . **Name:** ☐

3 Click . . . . ☐ OK ☐

Move Sheets within a Workbook

To move <u>one</u> sheet:

1 If necessary, click . . . . . *tab scrolling buttons* ⏮ ◀ ▶ ⏭
to scroll a hidden sheet tab into view.

2 Drag . . . . ⟍Sheet #⟋
where *Sheet #* is the name of sheet to move
to . . . . *desired sheet tab position*
Pointer becomes a 🖗*, and black triangle indicates point of insertion.*

To move <u>multiple</u> sheets:

1 If necessary, click . . . . . *tab scrolling buttons* ⏮ ◀ ▶ ⏭
to scroll a hidden sheet tab into view.

2 Select . . . . *sheets to move*

3 Drag . . . . *selected sheets*
to . . . . *desired sheet tab position*
Pointer changes to 🖗*, and black triangle indicates point of insertion.*

Move Sheets to Another Workbook

*NOTE: Excel will rename moved sheets when a sheet with the same name
exists in the destination workbook.*

1 Arrange . *workspace so that both workbooks are in view*

2 Select . . . . *sheet(s) to move*

3 Drag . . . . *selected sheet(s)*
to . . . . *a sheet tab position in destination workbook*
Pointer changes to 🖗 *or* 🖗*, and black triangle indicates
point of insertion.*
*NOTE: If you drag sheets to an empty workspace area,
Excel will create a new workbook for them.*

Copy Sheets within a Workbook

NOTE: *Excel will rename sheets that you copy.*

To copy <u>one</u> sheet:

1 If necessary, click . . . . . *tab scrolling buttons*

2 Press **Ctrl** and drag . . . . ⟍ Sheet # ⟋
where *Sheet #* is the name of sheet to copy
to . . . . *desired sheet tab position*
Pointer changes to ⬚, and black triangle indicates point of insertion.

To copy <u>multiple</u> sheets:

1 If necessary, click . . . . . *tab scrolling buttons*

2 Select . . . . *sheets to copy*

3 Press **Ctrl** and drag . . . . *selected sheets*
to . . . . *desired sheet tab position*
Pointer changes to ⬚, and black triangle indicates point of insertion.

Copy Sheets to Another Workbook

NOTE: *Excel will rename copied sheets when a sheet with the same name exists in the destination workbook.*

1 Arrange . . . . . *workspace so both workbooks are in view*

2 Select . . . . *sheet(s) to copy*

3 Press **Ctrl** and drag . . . . *selected sheet(s)*
to . . . . *a sheet tab position in destination workbook*
Pointer changes to ⬚ or ⬚, and black triangle indicates point of insertion.
NOTE: *If you drag sheets to an empty workspace area, Excel will create a new workbook for the sheets.*

Select Cells

(Also see Change Active Cell within Selection, page 47.)

To select <u>one</u> cell:

● Click . . . . *cell*

To select a <u>range</u> of cells:

● Drag through . . . . *adjacent cells*
until desired cells are highlighted.

To select a <u>multiple selection</u> of cells:

1 Click . . . . *first cell*

2 Press **Ctrl** and click . . . . *each additional cell*
AND/OR
Press **Ctrl** and drag through . . . . *adjacent cells*
until desired cells are highlighted.

To select <u>entire row or column</u>:

● Click . . . . *row heading* or *column heading*

To select <u>adjacent rows or columns</u>:

● Point to . . . . . *first row heading* or *first column heading*
<u>and</u> drag through . . . . *adjacent headings*
until desired rows or columns are highlighted.

To select <u>all cells</u> in worksheet:

● Click . . . . *Select All button*
located at intersection of row and column headings.

To <u>deselect</u> any cell selection:

● Click . . . . *any cell*

To select <u>a row or column in a data block</u>:
NOTE: A data block is a group of adjacent cells containing data.

1 Select . . . . *first cell(s) in block*

2 Point to . . . . *border of selected cell(s)*
in direction to extend selection.
Pointer becomes a ↖.

3 Press **Shift** and double-click . . . . *selection border*

Continued ...

Select Cells (continued)

To select a named reference from the Name Box:
(Also see Name Cell Reference, pages 83 and 84.)

- Select name in . . . . **Name Box** ⬚ ⬛
  to left of the formula bar.

To select a cell reference from the Name Box:

1 Click in . . . . **Name Box** ⬚ ⬛
  to left of the formula bar.

2 Type . . . . **cell reference**

3 Press . . . . ⏎
  *NOTE: You can also select specific cells by selecting Go To...
  from the Edit menu.*

To select (go to) a named or specific cell reference:

1 Press . . . . [F5]

2 Select reference name in . . . . **Go to** list

  OR

  Type cell reference in . . . . **Reference:** ⬚

3 Click . . . . [OK]

Select Visible Cells Only

Selects cells crossing over hidden rows or columns without selecting the hidden cells.

1 Select . . . . **cells that cross over the hidden cells**

2 Click . . . . **Edit, Go To...**

  OR

  Press . . . . [F5]

3 Click . . . . [Special...]

4 Select . . . . ○ **Visible** Cells Only

5 Click . . . . [OK]

44

Select Cells Containing Special Contents

1 Select . . . . *any cell to search entire worksheet*

OR

Select . . . . *cells to search*

2 Click . . . . **Edit, Go To...**

OR

Press **F5**

3 Click . . . . | Special... |

4 Select . . . . *Go To Special options:*
Notes, Constants (Numbers, Text, Logicals, Errors),
Formulas (Numbers, Text, Logicals, Errors), Blanks,
Current Region, Current Array, Row Differences,
Column Differences, Precedents (Direct Only, All Levels),
Dependents (Direct Only, All Levels), Last Cell, Visible Cells Only, Objects

NOTE: *If Precedents or Dependents was selected, Excel searches the entire worksheet.*

5 Click . . . . | OK |

Select Cells Containing Specific Data

1 Select . . . . *any cell to search entire worksheet*

OR

Select . . . . *cells to search*

OR

Select . . . . *sheets to search*
NOTE: *Excel searches all sheets in a group selection, except modules.*

2 Click . . . . **Edit, Find...**

Continued ...

Select Cells Containing Specific Data (continued)

3 Type characters to search for in ...... **Fi_n_d What:** [   ]

NOTE: You may use wildcard characters (and ?)
to represent any characters in a search. To find data
containing these special characters, you must type a tilde (~)
before them to tell Excel not to use them as wildcards.*

To specify a search direction:

• Select an option in .... **Search:** [⏷]
  *Search options include: By Columns, By Rows,
  (All, Down, Up (module sheets only))*

To look in specific places:

• Select an option in .... **Look in:** [⏷]
  *Look in options include: Formulas, Values, Notes,
  (Procedure, Module, All Modules, Selected Text (module sheets only))*

To make search case specific:

• Select .... ☐ **Match _C_ase**

To find cells that exactly match:

• Select .... ☐ **Find Entire Cells _O_nly**

To find entire words not characters that match:
(Module sheets only)

• Select .... ☐ **Find _W_hole Words Only**

To find characters that match if using a word pattern as the search criteria:
(Module sheets only)

• Select .... ☐ **_U_se Pattern Matching**

4 Click .... [**Find Next**]
Excel selects first cell meeting the search criteria.

5 Click .... [**Find Next**]
to find next cell matching the search criteria.
*NOTE: You can reverse the search direction if you
press **Shift** and click Find Next button.*

6 Repeat step **5**, as needed.

7 Click .... [**Close**]

Cell Selection Keys

To:	Press:
Select a single cell	⬍
Extend selection in direction of arrow	Shift + ⬍
Extend selection to beginning of row	Shift + Home
Extend selection to end of data block in direction of arrow	End, Shift + ⬍
Select entire current row	Shift + Space
Select entire current column	Ctrl + Space
Select first cell in current row	Home
Select cell in current row in last occupied column	End, ↵
Select first cell in worksheet	Ctrl + Home
Select last cell containing data in worksheet	Ctrl + End
Extend selection to first cell in worksheet	Ctrl + Shift + Home
Extend selection to last cell containing data in worksheet	Ctrl + Shift + End
Select entire worksheet	Ctrl + A
Select first or last cell in a horizontal data block* or select first or last cell in row	Ctrl + ← (first) or Ctrl + → (last)
Select first or last cell in a vertical data block* or select first or last cell in column	Ctrl + ↑ (first) or Ctrl + ↓ (last)
Extends selection to end of data block* in direction of arrow	Ctrl + Shift + ⬍
Extend selection to include entire data block*	Ctrl + Shift + *
Extend selection up one screen	Shift + PgUp
Extend selection down one screen	Shift + PgDn
Deselect a multiple selection, except active cell	Shift + BkSp

*A **data block** is a group of adjacent cells containing data.*

Change Active Cell within Selection

NOTES: *In a selection, only one cell can be active. When a cell is active, you can enter data in the cell.*

- Select . . . . ***cell range***
  Excel activates first cell in selection.

To activate any cell using mouse:

- Press **Ctrl** and click . . . . ***cell to activate***

To move active cell from top to bottom:

- Press . . . . ⏎
  NOTE: *If selection is a single row, moves active cell from left to right.*

To move active cell from bottom to top:

- Press . . . . **Shift** + ⏎
  NOTE: *If selection is a single row, moves active cell from right to left.*

To move active cell from left to right:

- Press . . . . **Tab**
  NOTE: *If selection is a single column, moves active cell from top to bottom.*

To move active cell from right to left:

- Press . . . . **Shift** + **Tab**
  NOTE: *If selection is in a single column, moves active cell from bottom to top.*

To move active cell to next corner of selection:

- Press . . . . **Ctrl** + **.**

To move active cell to first cell in next range in a multiple selection:

- Press . . . . **Ctrl** + **Alt** + →

To move active cell to first cell in previous range in a multiple selection:

- Press . . . . **Ctrl** + **Alt** + ←

Enter Text

NOTE: *Text cannot be calculated. By default, text is left-aligned.*

1 Select . . . . *cell(s) to receive text*

2 Type . . . . *text*

3 Enter . . . . ⏎

NOTE: *To have the text wrap in one cell, see **Wrap Text in a Cell**, page 141.*

Enter Numbers as Text

NOTE: *Numbers entered as text cannot be calculated. By default, numbers entered as text are left-aligned.*

1 Select . . . . *cell(s) to receive data*

2 Press . . . . '

3 Type . . . . *number*
   EXAMPLE: '1305

4 Enter . . . . ⏎

Enter Numbers as Values

NOTE: *Numbers can be calculated. By default, numbers are right-aligned.*

1 Select . . . . *cell(s) to receive numbers*

   To format the number as currency:

   • Press . . . . $

2 Type . . . . *number*
   NOTE: *Precede negative numbers with a minus sign (-), or enclose negative number within parentheses ().*

   To format the number as a percentage:

   • Press . . . . %

3 Enter . . . . ⏎

NOTES: *If Excel displays ######, column is not wide enough to display the date. To change column width, see **Change Column Widths**, page 136. To change the format, see **Format Number, Date or Time**, page 148.*

Enter Numbers as Fractions

NOTE: *Numbers can be calculated. By default, numbers are right-aligned.*

1 Select .... ***cell(s) to receive numbers***

2 Type Zero .... 0️⃣

3 Press .... Space

4 Type .... ***fraction***
Example: 0 1/4

5 Enter .... ⏎

NOTE: *If Excel displays ######, column is not wide enough to display the date. To change column width, see* **Change Column Widths,** *page 136.*

Enter Mixed Numbers

NOTE: *Numbers can be calculated. By default, numbers are right-aligned.*

1 Select .... ***cell(s) to receive numbers***

2 Type .... ***number***

3 Press .... Space

4 Type .... ***fraction***
Example: 5 1/4

5 Enter .... ⏎

NOTE: *If Excel displays ######, column is not wide enough to display the date. To change column width, see* **Change Column Widths,** *page 136.*

Enter a Date

NOTE: Date is a number and is right-aligned.

1 Select . . . . *cell to receive date*

To enter current date:

- Press . . . . **Ctrl** + **;**

To enter a specific date:

- Type . . . . *date in valid format*

  You may use the following formats:
  m/d/yy   (e.g. 6/24/52)
  d-mmm   (e.g. 24-Jun)
  d-mmm-yy   (e.g. 24-Jun-52)
  mmm-yy   (e.g. Jun-52)

2 Enter . . . . **⏎**

NOTES: *If Excel displays ######, column is not wide enough to display the date. To change column width, see* **Change Column Widths***, page 136. To change the date format, see* **Format Number, Date or Time***, page 148.*

Enter a Time

NOTE: Time is a number and is right-aligned.

1 Select . . . . *cell to receive time*

To enter current time:

- Press . . . . **Ctrl** + **Shift** + **:**

To enter a specific time:

- Type . . . . *time in a valid format*

  You may use the following formats:
  h:mm:ss AM/PM   (e.g. 1:55:25 PM)
  h:mm AM/PM   (e.g. 1:55 PM)
  h:mm   (e.g. 1:55)
  h:mm:ss   (e.g. 1:55:25)

2 Enter . . . . **⏎**

NOTES: *If Excel displays ######, column is not wide enough to display the date. To change column width, see* **Change Column Widths***, page 136. To change the time format, see* **Format Number, Date or Time***, page 148.*

Enter a Date and Time in One Cell

1 Select .... *cell to receive date and time*

2 Type .... *date in a valid format*
(m/d/yy – e.g. 6/24/52)

3 Press .... Space

4 Type .... *time in a valid format*
(h:mm – e.g. 1:55)

5 Enter .... ↵

Enter Identical Data in More than One Cell at a Time

1 Select .... *cells to receive data*

2 Type .... *data*

3 Press .... Ctrl + ↵
Excel enters data in all selected cells.

Enter Identical Data in More than One Worksheet at a Time

1 Select .... *sheets to receive data*

2 Type .... *data*
Excel enters data in same cells in all worksheets in group.

Cancel a Cell Entry Before it is Entered

• Click .... *Cancel button* ☒

 OR

 Press .... Esc

Set Up Workbook to Add Decimal Places or Zeros Automatically

NOTE: This setting changes the values you enter in cells. To override this setting, type the decimal point when you enter a number.

1 Click . . . . **Tools, Options...**

2 Click . . . . [Edit]

3 Select . . . . ☐ **Fixed Decimal**

4 Type or select number in . . . . **Places:** [⬍]

   NOTE: The number you specify tells Excel to add decimal places or zeros to the numbers you enter in a worksheet. A positive number sets Excel to move decimal to the left. A negative number sets Excel to move decimal to the right (add zeros to value).

5 Click . . . . [OK]

Set Edit Options

Sets defaults for entering, editing, copying, and moving data.

1 Click . . . . **Tools, Options...**

2 Click . . . . [Edit]

3 Select or deselect . . . . ***Settings options:***

   Edit Directly in Cell – select to allow editing of data in cells.
   Allow Cell Drag and Drop – select to move or copy cell contents by dragging.
   Alert before Overwriting Cells – to set confirmation before overwriting data.
   Move Selection after Enter – select to move active cell down after you press Enter.
   Fixed Decimal Places – (see above).
   Cut, Copy, and Sort Objects with Cells – select to keep objects with cells when you cut, copy, filter, or sort.
   Ask to Update Automatic Links – select to confirm update to links when a link exists.

4 Click . . . . [OK]

Enable Cell Editing

1 Double-click .... *cell to edit*

OR

  a Select .... *cell to edit*

  b Press .... [F2]

An insertion point appears in active cell and these buttons appear on formula bar:

☒ **Cancel button** – *cancels changes made in cell*

☑ **Enter button** – *accepts changes made in cell*

fx **Function Wizard button** – *starts Function Wizard.*

To edit the data in the formula bar:

* Click .... *anywhere in formula bar*

2 Edit .... *data*

Refer to the following procedures:

Select Data to Edit, *pages 53 and 54.*

Move Insertion Point in a Cell or Formula Bar, *page 55.*

Edit Cell Contents (Options) *page 56.*

Build a Formula, *page 79.*

3 Press .... [↵]

to accept changes

OR

Press .... [Esc]

to cancel changes.

Select Data to Edit (Using Mouse)

* Double-click .... *cell to edit*

*(Also see **Enable Cell Editing,** above.)*

To position insertion point:

* Click .... *desired data position*

To select a group of consecutive characters:

* Drag .... *highlight over characters*

To select a word or cell reference:

* Double-click .... *word* or *cell reference*

Select Data to Edit (Using Keyboard)

1 Double-click .... *cell to edit*
*(Also see **Enable Cell Editing**, page 53.)*

2 Press .... ⬍

<u>until</u> insertion point is in desired position.

To select one character left or right:
• Press .... Shift + ⬌

To extend selection one word left or right:
• Press .... Ctrl + Shift + ⬌

To extend selection to beginning of line:
• Press .... Shift + Home

To extend selection to end of line:
• Press .... Shift + End

To extend selection to beginning of data entry:
When entry includes more than one line of data.
• Press .... Ctrl + Shift + Home

To extend selection to end of data entry:
When entry includes more than one line of data.
• Press .... Ctrl + Shift + End

Move Insertion Point in a Cell or Formula Bar (Using Keyboard)

- Double-click .... ***cell to edit***
  *(Also see **Enable Cell Editing**, page 53.)*

  To move one character left or right:
  - Press .... ⬅️➡️

  To move one word left or right:
  - Press .... **Ctrl** + ⬅️➡️

  To move to beginning of line:
  - Press .... **Home**

  To move to end of line:
  - Press .... **End**

  To move to beginning of data entry:
  When entry includes more than one line of data.
  - Press .... **Ctrl** + **Home**

  To move to end of data entry:
  When entry includes more than one line of data.
  - Press .... **Ctrl** + **End**

Edit Cell Contents (Options)

- Double-click . . . . *cell to edit*
  (Also see Enable Cell Editing, page 53.)

To delete character to right of insertion point:
- Press . . . . **Del**

To delete character to left of insertion point:
- Press . . . . **BkSp**

To delete selected data:
- Press . . . . **Del**

To delete to end of line:
When entry includes more than one line of data.

- Press . . . . **Ctrl** + **Del**

To copy selected data to Clipboard:
- Click . . . . *Copy button* 🖺
  on Standard toolbar.

  OR

  Press . . . . **Ctrl** + **C**

To delete selected data and transfer to Clipboard:
- Click . . . . *Cut button* ✂
  on Standard toolbar.

  OR

  Press . . . . **Ctrl** + **X**

To paste Clipboard data at insertion point:
- Click . . . . *Paste button* 📋
  on Standard toolbar.

  OR

  Press . . . . **Ctrl** + **V**

To insert a line break at insertion point:
- Press . . . . **Alt** + **↵**

Move Cell Contents (Using Toolbar)

1 Select .... *cell(s) to move*

2 Click .... *Cut button* ✂
on Standard toolbar.
A flashing outline surrounds selection.

To change destination workbook or worksheet:

• Select .... *workbook* and/or *sheet*

3 Select .... *destination cell(s)*
*NOTE: Select an area the same shape as the area to move,
or select the upper left cell in the destination cell range.*

To move and <u>overwrite</u> existing data in destination cells:

• Enter .... ⏎

To move and <u>insert</u> between existing cells:

a Right-click .... *any destination cell*

b Click .... **Insert Cut Cells**

b If prompted, select .... *Insert Paste option:*
Shift Cells Right, Shift Cells Down

c Click .... OK

Move Cell Contents (by Dragging)

1 Select .... *cell(s) to move*

2 Point to .... *any border of selected cells*
Pointer becomes a ↖.

To move and <u>overwrite</u> existing data in destination cells:

a Drag .... *border outline to new location*

b Click .... OK

To move and <u>insert</u> between existing cells:

a Press Shift and drag .... *insertion outline*
onto .... *row gridline* or *column gridline*

b Release .... *mouse button, then the key*

Move Cell Contents (Using Menu)

1 Select . . . . *cell(s) to move*

2 Click . . . . **Edit, Cut**
A flashing outline surrounds selection.

To change destination workbook or worksheet:

• Select . . . . *workbook* and/or *sheet*

3 Select . . . . *destination cell(s)*
NOTE: *Select an area the same shape as the area to move,
or select the upper left cell in the destination cell range.*

To move and <u>overwrite</u> existing data in destination cells:

• Enter . . . . ⏎

To move and <u>insert</u> between existing cells:

a Click . . . . **Insert, Cut Cells**

b If prompted, select . . . . **Insert Paste option:**
Shift Cells Right, Shift Cells Down

c Click . . . . OK

Move Cell Contents (Using Shortcut Menu)

1 Select .... *cell(s) to move*

2 Right-click .... *any cell in selection*

3 Click .... **Cut**
A flashing outline surrounds selection.

To change destination workbook or worksheet:

• Select .... *workbook* and/or *sheet*

4 Select .... *destination cell(s)*
NOTE: *Select an area the same shape as the area to move, or select the upper left cell in the destination cell range.*

To move and <u>overwrite</u> existing data in destination cells:

• Enter .... ⏎

To move and <u>insert</u> between existing cells:

a Right-click .... *any destination cell*

b Click .... **Insert Cut Cells**

c If prompted, select .... **Insert Paste option:**
Shift Cells Right, Shift Cells Down

d Click .... OK

Move or Copy Cell Contents (by Dragging with Right Mouse Button)

1 Select .... *cell(s) to move or copy*

2 Point to .... *any border of selected cells*
Pointer becomes a .

3 Press right mouse button
and drag .... *border outline to new location*

4 Select .... *shortcut menu option:*
Copy (overwrite), Move (overwrite), Copy Formats, Copy Values, Shift Down and Copy, Shift Right and Copy, Shift Down and Move, Shift Right and Move

Copy Cell Contents (Using Toolbar)

CAUTION: This copy procedure overwrites existing data in destination cells.

1 Select . . . . ***cell(s) to copy***

2 Click . . . . ***Copy button*** 📋
on Standard toolbar.
A flashing outline surrounds selection.

To change destination workbook or worksheet:

• Select . . . . ***workbook*** and/or ***sheet***

3 Select . . . . ***destination cell(s)***
NOTE: *Select an area the same size as the area to copy,*
or select the upper left cell in the destination cell range.
To copy to multiple areas, press **Ctrl** *and click upper left*
cell in each destination area.

To copy once:

• Enter . . . . ↵

To copy with option to repeat copy:

a Click . . . . ***Paste button*** 📋
on Standard toolbar.

To repeat copy:

1. Click . . . . ***upper left cell in destination area***

2. Click . . . . ***Paste button*** 📋

3. Repeat steps **1** and **2** for each copy to make.

b Press . . . . Esc
to end copying.

Copy Cell Contents (Using Menu)

1 Select .... *cell(s) to copy*
2 Click .... **Edit, Copy**
A flashing outline surrounds selection.

To change destination workbook or worksheet:

• Select .... *workbook* and/or *sheet*

3 Select .... *destination cell(s)*
NOTE: Select an area the same size as the area to copy,
or select the upper left cell in the destination cell range.
*To copy to multiple areas, press **Ctrl** and click upper left*
cell in each destination area.

To copy once and <u>overwrite</u> existing data in destination cells:

• Enter .... ⏎

To copy (with option to repeat copy) and <u>overwrite</u> existing data in destination cells:

a Click .... **Edit, Paste**
To repeat copy:

  1. Click .... *upper left cell in destination area*
  2. Click .... **Edit, Paste**
  3. Repeat steps 1 and 2 for each copy to make.

b Press .... Esc
to end copying.

To copy and <u>insert</u> between existing cells:

a Click .... **Insert, Copied Cells**
b If prompted, select .... *Insert Paste option:*
Shift Cells Right, Shift Cells Down
c Click .... OK
d Press .... Esc
to end copying.

Copy Cell Contents (Using Shortcut Menu)

1 Select . . . . *cell(s) to copy*

2 Right-click . . . . *any cell in selection*

3 Click . . . . **Copy**
A flashing outline surrounds selection.

To change destination workbook or worksheet:

• Select . . . . *workbook* and/or *sheet*

4 Select . . . . *destination cell(s)*
NOTE: *Select an area the same shape as the area to copy,
or select the upper left cell in the destination cell range.
To copy to multiple areas, press* **Ctrl** *and click upper left
cell in each destination area.*

To copy once and <u>overwrite</u> existing data in destination cells:

• Enter 	⏎

To copy (with option to repeat copy) and <u>overwrite</u> any data in destination cells:

a Right-click . . . . *any destination cell*

To repeat copy:

  1. Click . . . . *upper left cell in destination area*

  2. Click . . . . **Paste**

  3. Repeat steps **1** and **2** for each copy to make.

b Press 	Esc
to end copying.

To copy and <u>insert</u> between existing cells:

a Right-click . . . . *any destination cell*

b Click . . . . **Insert Copied Cells**

c If prompted, select . . . . **Insert Paste option:**
Shift Cells Right, Shift Cells Down

d Click 	OK

e Press 	Esc
to end copying.

Copy Cell Contents (by Dragging)

1 Select . . . . *cell(s) to copy*

2 Point to . . . . *any border of selected cells*
Pointer becomes a ⬉.

To copy and <u>overwrite</u> existing data in destination cells:

a Press **Ctrl** and drag . . . . *border outline to new location*

b Release . . . . *mouse button, then the key*

c Click . . . . `  OK  `

To copy and <u>insert</u> between existing cells:

a Press **Ctrl+Shift** and drag . . . . *insertion outline*
onto . . . . *row gridline* or *column gridline*

b Release . . . . *mouse button, then the keys*

Copy and Fill Adjacent Cells (Using Fill Handle)

CAUTION: This procedure overwrites existing data in destination area.
NOTE: If Excel recognizes a pattern (series) in the cells to copy, it does not copy the data but extends the pattern into the destination area.

1 Select . . . . *cell(s) to copy*

2 Point to . . . . *fill handle*
(Small square in lower right corner of selection.)
Pointer becomes a ✛.

*NOTE: To prevent a series from being extended, you must press **Ctrl** while executing step 3.*

3 Drag . . . . ✛
to extend border over adjacent cells in rows or columns to fill.

CAUTION: Dragging ✛ over selected cells will delete the data. If you do this, you can click Edit, Undo to undelete the data.

Fill Cells with Contents of Selected Cells (Using Menu)

Copies cell contents and formats from a specified side of selected cells into remaining part of selection.
CAUTION: *This procedure overwrites existing data in destination cells.*

- Select . . . . **cell(s) to copy and destination cell(s)**
  NOTE: *Destination cells must be in the same row or column as cells containing data to copy.*

To fill columns to the right with data from the left column:

a Click . . . . **Edit, Fill** ►

b Click . . . . **Right**

To fill rows below with data from the top row:

a Click . . . . **Edit, Fill** ►

b Click . . . . **Down**

To fill columns to the left with data from right column:

a Click . . . . **Edit, Fill** ►

b Click . . . . **Left**

To fill rows above with data from bottom row:

a Click . . . . **Edit, Fill** ►

b Click . . . . **Up**

Copy Specific Cell Contents

Copies formulas, values, formats, or notes.

1 Select .... *cell(s) to copy*

2 Click .... **Edit, Copy**

  OR

  a Right-click .... *any cell in selection*

  b Click .... **Copy**

  A flashing outline surrounds selection.

To change destination workbook or worksheet:

  • Select .... *workbook* and/or *sheet*

3 Select .... *destination cell(s)*

  NOTE: *Select an area the same shape as the area to copy,*
  or select the upper left cell in the destination cell range.
  To copy to multiple areas, press **Ctrl** *and click upper left*
  cell in each destination area.

4 Click .... **Edit, Paste Special...**

  OR

  a Right-click .... *any destination cell*

  b Click .... **Paste Special...**

5 Select .... *Paste option:*
  All, Formulas, Values, Formats, Notes

6 Click .... OK

Copy Formulas or Values and Combine with Data in Destination Cells

1   Select . . . . *cell(s) to copy*

2   Click . . . . **Edit, Copy**

     OR

     a   Right-click . . . . *any cell in selection*

     b   Click . . . . **Copy**

     A flashing outline surrounds selection.

To change destination workbook or worksheet:

     •   Select . . . . *workbook* and/or *sheet*

3   Select . . . . *destination cell(s)*

     NOTE: Select an area the same shape as the area to copy,
     or select the upper left cell in the destination cell range.
     To copy to multiple areas, press **Ctrl** *and click upper left*
     cell in each destination area.

4   Click . . . . **Edit, Paste Special...**

     OR

     a   Right-click . . . . *any destination cell*

     b   Click . . . . **Paste Special...**

5   Select . . . . ◯ **Formulas** or ◯ **Values**
     to set what type of data will be combined.

6   Select . . . . *Operation option:*
     to set how copied data will be combined.
     None, Add, Subtract, Multiply, Divide
     NOTE: Select None to overwrite existing data in the destination cells.

7   Click . . . . `OK`

8   Press . . . . `Esc`
     to end copying.

Copy and Change Orientation of Data (Transpose)

Changes orientation of copied cells from rows to columns or from columns to rows.

1 Select . . . . *cell(s) to copy*

2 Click . . . . **Edit, Copy**

OR

   a Right-click . . . . *any cell in selection*

   b Click . . . . **Copy**

A flashing outline surrounds selection.

To change destination workbook or worksheet:

- Select . . . . *workbook* and/or *sheet*

3 Select . . . . *upper left cell in destination area*

NOTE: *To copy to multiple areas, press **Ctrl** and click upper left cell in each destination area. The destination cell area and the area of the cells to copy cannot overlap.*

4 Click . . . . **Edit, Paste Special...**

OR

   a Right-click . . . . *any destination cell*

   b Click . . . . **Paste Special...**

5 Select . . . . ☐ **Transpose**

6 Click . . . . `OK`

7 Press . . . . **Esc**
to end copying.

Copy Only Occupied Cells

Prevents any blank cells in cells to copy from overwriting data in the destination cells.

1 Select . . . . *cell(s) to copy*

2 Click . . . . **Edit, Copy**

OR

   a Right-click . . . . *any cell in selection*

   b Click . . . . **Copy**

A flashing outline surrounds selection.

To change destination workbook or worksheet:

   • Select . . . . *workbook* and/or *sheet*

3 Select . . . . *destination cell(s)*

*NOTE: Select an area the same shape as the area to copy, or select the upper left cell in the destination cell range. To copy to multiple areas, press **Ctrl** and click upper left cell in each destination area.*

4 Click . . . . **Edit, Paste Special...**

OR

   a Right-click . . . . *any destination cell*

   b Click . . . . **Paste Special...**

5 Select . . . . ☐ **Skip Blanks**

6 Click . . . . `OK`

7 Press . . . . `Esc`

to end copying.

Clear Cell Options (Using Menu)

Removes the formats, contents (data and formulas), notes, or all the above, and leaves the cells blank in the worksheet. When cleared cells are referenced by formulas, they return a value of zero.

1 Select . . . . *cell(s) to clear*

2 Click . . . .**Edit, Clear** ►

3 Select . . . . *Clear option:*
  All, Formats, Contents, Notes

Clear Cell Contents

Removes the contents (data and formulas) and leaves the cells blank in the worksheet. When cleared cells are referenced by formulas, they return a value of zero.

1 Select . . . . *cell(s) to clear*

2 Press . . . . Del

  OR

  a Right-click . . . . *any selected cell*

  b Click . . . . **Clear Contents**

Clear Cells (by Dragging)

Removes the formats, contents (data and formulas), notes, or all the above, and leaves the cells blank in the worksheet. When cleared cells are referenced by formulas, they return a value of zero.

1 Select . . . . *cell(s) to clear*

2 Point to . . . . *fill handle*
  Pointer becomes a ╋.

  NOTE: *The fill handle is small square in lower right corner of a cell selection.*

To clear cell contents:

  • Drag . . . . ╋ *over selection*

Continued ...

Clear Cells — by Dragging (continued)

To clear cell contents, formats, and notes:
a Press **Ctrl** and drag . . . . ╅ *over selection*

b Release . . . . *mouse button, then the key*

Delete Cells (Using Menu)

Removes the cells from the worksheet. Adjacent cells are shifted to close the space left by the deletion. When deleted cells are referenced by a formula, the formula will show a #REF! error message.

1 Select . . . . *cell(s) to delete*

2 Click . . . . **Edit, Delete...**

OR

   a Right-click . . . . *any cell in selection*

   b Click . . . . **Delete...**

3 Select . . . . **Delete option:**
Shift Cells Left, Shift Cells Up, Entire Row, Entire Column

4 Click . . . . `  OK  `

Delete Rows or Columns (Using Menu)

NOTE: *Deleting removes the rows or columns from the worksheet and shifts adjacent rows or columns into the space left by the deletion. When cells in the deleted rows or columns are referenced, a formula will show a #REF! error message.*

1 Select . . . . *rows or columns to delete*

2 Click . . . . **Edit, Delete**

OR

   a Right-click . . . . *any cell in selection*

   b Click . . . . **Delete**

Delete Cells, Rows or Columns (by Dragging)

Removes the cells, rows, or columns from the worksheet. Adjacent cells are shifted to close the space left by the deletion. When deleted cells are referenced by a formula, the formula will show a #REF! error message.

1 Select . . . . *cell(s), row(s), or column(s) to delete*

2 Point to . . . . *fill handle*
Pointer becomes a $+$.

> **NOTE:** *The fill handle is small square in the lower right corner of a cell selection. The fill handle for selected row or column is located in the lower right corner of the row or column heading.*

3 Press **Shift** and drag . . . . $\Leftrightarrow$ or $\Leftrightarrow$ *over selection*

4 Release . . . . *mouse button, then the key*

Insert Blank Cells (Using Menu)

> **NOTE:** *Existing data is shifted to make room for inserted cells. Excel adjusts references to shifted cells.*

1 Select . . . . *cell(s) where insertion will occur*
> **NOTE:** *Select the same number of cells as the blank cells to insert.*

2 Click . . . . **Insert, Cells...**
   OR
   a Right-click . . . . *any cell in selection*
   b Click . . . . **Insert...**

3 Select . . . . *Insert option:*
Shift Cells Right, Shift Cells Down, Entire Row, Entire Column

4 Click . . . . ☐ OK

Insert Blank Rows or Columns (Using Menu)

NOTE: Existing data is shifted to make room for inserted columns or rows. Excel adjusts references to shifted cells.

1 Select . . . . . . ***rows or columns where insertion will occur***
   NOTE: Select the number of rows or columns you want to insert.

2 Click . . . . **Insert, Rows** or **Insert, Columns**
   OR
   a Right-click . . . . ***any selected cell***
   b Click . . . . **Insert**

Insert Blank Cells, Rows or Columns (by Dragging)

NOTE: Existing data is shifted to make room for inserted cells. Excel adjusts references to shifted cells.

1 Select . . . . ***cell(s)***
   above and to the left of where insertion will occur.
   NOTE: Select the number of cells you want to insert.

   OR

   Select . . . . ***row(s)*** or ***column(s)***
   where insertion will occur.
   NOTE: Select the number of rows or columns you want to insert.

2 Point to . . . . ***fill handle***
   Pointer becomes a +.

   NOTE: The fill handle is small square in the lower right corner of a cell selection. The fill handle for selected row or column is located in the lower right corner of the row or column heading.

3 Press **Shift** and drag . . . . . ⇕ or ⇔ ***down or to the right***
   to extend border outside selection.

4 Release . . . . ***mouse button, then the key***

Create a Series of Numbers, Dates, or Times (Using Menu)

1 Enter . . . . *first series value in consecutive cells*
to base series on a single value.

OR

Enter . . *first and second series values in consecutive cells*
to base series on multiple values.

2 Select . . . . . *cells containing series values <u>and</u> cells to fill*
NOTE: Select adjacent cells in rows or columns to fill.

3 Click . . . . <u>E</u>dit, F<u>i</u>ll ►

4 Click . . . . **Series...**

To change proposed direction of series:

● Select . . . . *Series in option:*
<u>R</u>ows, <u>C</u>olumns

To change proposed series type:

● Select . . . . *Type option:*
<u>L</u>inear – to increase/decrease each value in series by number
in Step Value text box.
<u>G</u>rowth – to multiply each value in series by number in Step
Value text box.
<u>D</u>ate – to set increment by days weekdays months or years.
Auto<u>F</u>ill – to fill cells based on values in selection.

If Date was selected,

● Select . . . . *Date Unit option:*
<u>D</u>ay, <u>W</u>eekday, <u>M</u>onth, <u>Y</u>ear

To change proposed step value:

● Type a number in . . . . **Step Value:** ▢

To set stop value for series:

● Type a number in . . . . **St<u>o</u>p Value:** ▢

5 Click . . . . ▢ OK

74   *Edit Cells*

Create a Series of Numbers (by Dragging with Right Mouse Button)

1   Enter . . . . *first series value in consecutive cells*
to base series on a single value.

OR

Enter . . *first and second series values in consecutive cells*
to base series on multiple values.

2   Select . . . . *cells containing series values*

3   Point to . . . . *fill handle*
Pointer becomes a ✛ *when positioned correctly on the fill handle.*

4   Press and hold . . . . *right mouse button*
Pointer becomes an ↳.
and drag . . . . *cell border*
in direction to extend series in.
*NOTE: Drag border down, or to the right, to create an ascending
series. Drag border up, or to the left, to create a descending series.*

5   Select . . . . *shortcut menu option:*
*Fill Series, Fill Formats, Fill Values, Fill Days, Fill Weekdays, Fill Months,
Fill Years, Linear Trend, Growth Trend, Series...*

If Series was selected,

● Follow steps below step **4** in **Create a Series of Numbers,
Dates or Times (Using Menu)**, page 73.

Create a Series of Numbers, Dates, or Times (by Dragging)

1 Enter . . . . *first series value in consecutive cells*
to base series on a single value.

OR

Enter . . *first and second series values in consecutive cells*
to base series on multiple values.

2 Select . . . . *cells containing series value(s)*

3 Point to . . . . *fill handle*
<u>and</u> drag . . . . ╋ *over adjacent cells*
to extend border in rows or columns to fill.

NOTES: Fill handle is small square in lower right corner of selection.
Drag ╋ down or to the right to increase values, or drag ╋ up or to
the left to decrease values.

You can create a series from a value in a single cell by pressing **Ctrl**
while dragging ╋⁺ to extend cell border over adjacent cells.

Spell Check

1 Select . . . . *any cell*
NOTE: This selection spell checks all cells, headers, footers,
embedded charts, text boxes, cell notes, and text in buttons.

OR

Select . . . . *cells to spell check*

OR

Select . . . . *sheets to spell check*
NOTE: Excel spell checks all sheets in a group except modules.

OR

Select . . . . *word* or *phrase* or *object*

2 Click . . . . *Spelling button* 🔤
on Standard toolbar.

OR

Click . . . . <u>T</u>ools, <u>S</u>pelling...

Continued ...

Spell Check (continued)

To <u>replace</u> word not found in dictionary with suggested word:

a Type replacement word in . . . . **Change To:** [_____]

OR

Select word in . . . . **Suggestions** list

b Click . . . . [Change]
to replace only current instance.
OR
Click . . . . [Change All]
to replace all instances.

To undo last change:

• Click . . . . [Undo Last]

To <u>skip</u> word not found in dictionary:

• Click . . . . [Ignore]
to skip only current instance.
OR
Click . . . . [Ignore All]
to skip all instances.

To <u>add</u> word not found to current dictionary:

• Click . . . . [Add]

To ignore uppercase words:

• Select . . . . □ **Ignore UPPERCASE**

To end spell checking:

• Click . . . . [Cancel]
OR
Click . . . . [Close]

3 Click . . . . [OK]

Find and Replace Data

1 Select . . . . *any cell to search entire worksheet*
OR

Select . . . . *cells to search*
OR

Select . . . . *sheets to search*
NOTE: *Excel will search all sheets in a group except modules.*

2 Click . . . . **Edit, Replace...**

3 Type characters to search for in . . . . . . **Find What:** ☐

NOTE: *You may use wildcard characters (* and ?)
to represent any characters in a search. To find data
containing these special characters, you must type a tilde (~)
before them to tell Excel not to use them as wildcards.*

4 Type replacement characters in . . . . . **Replace with:** ☐

To specify a search direction:

- Select an option in . . . . **Search:** ☐
  *Search options include: By Columns, By Rows,
  (All, Down, Up (module sheets only))*

To make search case specific:

- Select . . . . ☐ **Match Case**

To find cells that match exactly:

- Select . . . . ☐ **Find Entire Cells Only**

To look in specific places:
(Module sheets only)

- Select an option in . . . . **Look in:** ☐
  *Look in options include: Procedure, Module, All Modules,
  Selected Text*

To set search to find entire words:
(Module sheets only)

- Select . . . . ☐ **Find Whole Words Only**

Continued ...

Find and Replace Data (continued)

To set search for pattern matching:
(Module sheets only)

- Select .... ☐ **Use Pattern Matching**

5 Click .... **Find Next**

Excel selects first cell meeting the search criteria.

6 Select .... *one of the following:*

To globally replace cell contents:

- Click .... **Replace All**

Excel replaces all matches and returns you to normal operations.

To selectively replace cell contents:

a Click .... **Replace**

to replace contents of active cell and find next match.

OR

Click .... **Find Next**

to retain contents of active cell and find next match.

*NOTE: You can reverse the search direction if you press **Shift** and click Find Next button.*

b Repeat step **a** for each item found.

c Click .... **Close**

to close Replace dialog box.

Type New Formula

1 Select .... *cell to receive formula*

2 Press .... 🔲
Equal sign appears in formula bar and cell.

3 Type .... *formula*
EXAMPLES: `=A1*(B2:B10)/2` `=SUM(A1:A10)*5`

NOTE: *For information about inserting references and functions into a formula, see **Build a Formula**, below.*

4 Enter .... ⏎

Build a Formula

Use these procedures to insert the following into a formula:
- *A **cell reference** from any workbook or worksheet.*
- *A **named reference**.*
- *A **named formula**.*
- *A **function** (using the Function Wizard).*

To insert a <u>cell reference</u>:

1 If necessary, type or edit .... *formula*
*(See **Type New Formula**, above, and **Enable Cell Editing**, page 53.)*

2 Place .... *insertion point in formula*
where reference will be inserted.
NOTE: *If necessary, type preceding operator or left parenthesis [(].*

3 If necessary, select .... *workbook* and/or *sheet*
containing cells to reference.
NOTE: *When you select a cell in another workbook, Excel creates a link to that workbook.*

4 Select .... *cell or cell range to insert in formula*
Reference appears in formula bar and cell.

To enter a 3-D reference for a range of worksheets:

- Press **Shift** and click .. *last worksheet tab to reference*

5 Type or build .... *remaining parts of formula*
OR
Enter .... ⏎

Continued ...

Build a Formula (continued)

To insert a <u>named reference</u> or <u>named formula</u>:

1 If necessary, type or edit . . . . *formula*
(See **Type New Formula**, page 79, and **Enable Cell Editing**, page 53.)

2 Place . . . . *insertion point*
where named reference or named formula will be inserted.
NOTE: If necessary, type preceding operator or left parenthesis [(].

3 **a** Click . . . . **<u>I</u>nsert, <u>N</u>ame, <u>P</u>aste...**

   b Select reference or formula name in . . . . **Paste <u>N</u>ame** list

   OR

   a Press F5 (Go to) . . . . |F5|

   b Select reference in . . . . **<u>G</u>o to** list

4 Click . . . . | OK |

5 Type or build . . . . *remaining parts of formula*

   OR

   Enter . . . . |↵|

To insert a <u>worksheet function</u> using Function Wizard

NOTE: You can also insert a function by selecting, <u>F</u>unction... from the <u>I</u>nsert menu.

1 If necessary, type or edit . . . . *formula*
(See **Type New Formula**, page 79, and **Enable Cell Editing**, page 53.)

2 Place . . . . *insertion point*
where function will be inserted.

3 Click . . . . |*fx*|
on formula bar.

Function Wizard – Step 1 of 2

4 Select a category in . . . . **Function <u>C</u>ategory** list

5 Select a function in . . . . **Function <u>N</u>ame** list

Continued ...

Build a Formula (continued)

6 Click . . . .   Next >

Function Wizard – Step 2 of 2

7 Type or insert arguments in . . . . **argument boxes**

NOTE: *An argument is data you supply to a function
so it can perform its operation.*

Depending on the function, you enter the following kinds of data:

numbers (constants) – *you can type numbers (integers, fractions,
mixed numbers, negative numbers) as you would in a cell.*
references – *you can type or insert references (page 79).*
named references or formulas – *you can type or insert named
references or formulas (pages 79 and 80).*
functions – *you can type a function or click* f_x *(to left of argument box)
to insert a function into an argument (nest functions).*

*The Function Wizard describes the current argument, indicates if
the argument is required, and shows you the result of the values
you have supplied.*

8 Click . . . .   Finish

9 Type or build . . . . **remaining parts of formula**

OR

Enter . . . . ⏎

Edit Worksheet Functions (Using Function Wizard)

1 Select . . . . *cell containing function(s)*

   NOTE: *Do not double-click cell.*

2 Click . . . . $\boxed{f_*}$
   on Standard toolbar.

   OR

   Press . . . . $\boxed{\text{Shift}}$ + $\boxed{\text{F3}}$

3 Edit or add arguments in . . . . *argument boxes*

   NOTE: *An argument is data you supply to a function so it can perform its operation.*

   Depending on the function, you enter the following kinds of data:

   numbers (constants) – *you can type numbers (integers, fractions, mixed numbers, negative numbers) as you would in a cell.*
   references – *you can type or insert references (page 79).*
   named references or formulas – *you can type or insert named references or formulas (pages 79 and 80).*
   functions – *you can type a function or click* $\boxed{f_*}$ *(to left of argument box) to insert a function into an argument (nest functions).*

   The Function Wizard describes the current argument, indicates if the argument is required, and shows you the result of the values you have supplied.

   ## To edit next or previous function in cell:

   a Click . . . . $\boxed{\text{Next >}}$ or $\boxed{\text{< Back}}$

   b Edit or add arguments in . . . . *argument boxes*

   c Repeat steps **a** and **b**, as needed.

4 Click . . . . $\boxed{\text{Finish}}$

Using Text in Titles to Name Cells

NOTE: You must convert titles that are numbers to text. Excel converts date values to text automatically. Spaces in text are replaced with underscore characters in the reference name.

1 Select . . . . *cells containing titles for names*
   and extend . . . . *selection*
   to include cells to name.

2 Click . . . . **Insert, Name** ▸, **Create...**

3 Select . . . . *Create Names in option:*
   Top Row, Left Column, Bottom Row, Right Column

4 Click . . . . [OK]

Name Cell Reference (Using Menu)

1 Select . . . . *cell(s) to name*

2 Click . . . . **Insert, Name** ▸, **Define...**
   OR
   Press . . . . [Ctrl] + [F3]

3 Type a name in . . . . **Names in Workbook:** [   ]
   NOTE: To create a sheet-level reference, precede reference name with the sheet name followed by an exclamation point (!).
   EXAMPLE: SHEET1!expenses

To change reference the name refers to:

a Click in . . . . **Refers to:** [   ]

b If necessary, delete . . . . *all or part of reference*

c Select . . . . *cells in worksheet to reference*
   OR
   Type . . . . *new reference*
   NOTE: Precede reference with an equal sign (=).

To add another named reference:

a Click . . . . [Add]

b Repeat step 3, then change reference the name refers to.

4 Click . . . . [OK]

84

Name Cells and Formulas

Name Cell Reference (Using Name Box)

1 Select . . . . **cell(s) to name**
2 Click in . . . . **Name box** ☐ ±
   on left side of formula bar.
3 Type . . . . **name for selected cell(s)**
4 Enter . . . . ⏎

Name Formula or Value

1 Click . . . . **Insert, Name** ▸, **Define...**
   OR
   Press . . . . **Ctrl** + **F3**
2 Type a name in . . . . **Names in Workbook:** ☐
3 Click in . . . . **Refers to:** ☐
4 Delete . . . . **existing reference**
   NOTE: *By default, Excel enters cell reference to selected cells in Refers to box.*
5 Type . . . . **formula** or **value**
   NOTE: *Precede formula or value with an equal sign (=). Formula may be pasted from the Clipboard. Cell references may be entered in formula by selecting cells in worksheet.*

   ### To add another named formula or value:
   a Click . . . . [Add]
   b Repeat steps 2-5.
6 Click . . . . [OK]

Edit or View Named Cell Reference or Named Formula

1 Click . . . . **Insert, Name** ►, **Define...**

2 Select name to edit or view in . . . . **Names in Workbook** list
Reference or formula appears in Refers to text box.

To change the name:

a Type new name in . . . . **Names in Workbook:** ⬚

b Click . . . . ⬚ Add

c Select old name in . . . . **Names in Workbook** list

d Click . . . . ⬚ Delete

To change reference the name refers to:

a Click in . . . . **Refers to:** ⬚

b If necessary, delete . . . . *all or part of reference*

c Select . . . . *cells in worksheet to reference*

OR

Type . . . . *new reference*
NOTE: *Precede reference with an equal sign (=).*

To change a named formula or value:

a Click in . . . . **Refers to:** ⬚

b Edit . . . . *formula* or *value*
NOTE: *Precede formula or value with an equal sign (=).*
Formula may be pasted from the Clipboard. Cell references may be entered in formula by selecting cells in worksheet.

3 Click . . . . ⬚ OK

List All Names and Their References

1 Select . . . . *upper left cell*
where list will be displayed.
CAUTION: *The list will overwrite existing data in destination area.*

2 Click . . . . **Insert, Name** ►, **Paste...**

3 Click . . . . ⬚ Paste List

Replace References with Defined Names

Excel searches worksheet for references that have been given names (pages 83 and 84) and replaces the references with the names.

1 Select .... **any cell**
   to replace all references with names in worksheet.

   OR

   Select .... **cells containing reference to replace**

2 Click .... **Insert, Name ►, Apply...**

3 Select names in .... **Apply Names** list

4 Select or deselect .... **options:**
   Ignore Relative/Absolute, Use Row and Column Names

   ## To set other options:

   a Click .... | Options >> |

   b Select or deselect .... **Apply Names options:**
      *Omit Column Name if Same Column, Omit Row Name if Same Row,
      Name Order – Row Column, Column Row*

5 Click .... | OK |

Delete Named Cell References or Named Formulas

NOTE: Excel will display #NAME? error message in cells containing formulas referring to a deleted name.

1 Click .... **Insert, Name ►, Define...**

2 Select name to delete in .... **Names in Workbook** list

3 Click .... | Delete |

4 Repeat steps 2 and 3, as needed.

5 Click .... | OK |

Use AutoSum

1 Select .... *cell(s) to receive sum(s)*
NOTE: *Select blank cell(s) below or to the right of cells containing values to total.*

To automatically calculate grand totals:

• Select .... *cells that include subtotals*
   and ... *a blank row and/or column adjacent to range*

2 Click .... *AutoSum button* $\boxed{\Sigma}$
on Standard toolbar.

OR

Press .... $\boxed{Alt}$+$\boxed{=}$

Excel inserts =SUM( ) function in formula bar, and a flashing outline may surround cells to be totaled.

To change proposed range to total:

• Select .... *cells to total*
3 If necessary, press .... $\boxed{↵}$
to add numbers.

88

Calculate

Set Calculation Options

Sets how worksheets and workbooks are calculated.

1 Click . . . . **Tools, Options...**

2 Click . . . . [Calculation]

To set <u>worksheet</u> calculation options:

- Select . . . . *Calculation option:*
  <u>A</u>utomatic, Automatic Except <u>T</u>ables, <u>M</u>anual

  If Manual,

  - Select or deselect . . . . ☐ **Recal<u>c</u>ulate before Save**
    Deselect to reduce time it takes to save a workbook.

To set <u>current workbook</u> calculation options:

- Select or deselect . . . . *Workbook options:*
  *Update <u>R</u>emote References – select to set Excel to calculate formulas
    containing references to other workbooks.*
  *<u>P</u>recision as Displayed – select to calculate values as displayed
    instead of how they are stored.*
  *1904 <u>D</u>ate System – select to set Excel to use Macintosh (1904) date
    system. Otherwise, Excel uses Windows (1900) date system.*
  *Save External <u>L</u>ink Values – select to reduce the time it takes to load
    a workbook containing links to other workbooks.*

To set goal seeking iteration limits or to resolve circular references:

a Select . . . . ☐ **Iteration**

b Type a number in . . . . . . **Maximum I<u>t</u>erations:** [ ]

c Type number in . . . . **Maximum <u>C</u>hange:** [ ]
   to set maximum change between iterations.

3 Enter . . . . ⏎

Calculate Only Selected Worksheet (When Calculation is Set to Manual)

Also updates charts embedded in worksheet and open chart sheets linked to worksheet.

1 Select .... ***worksheet to calculate***

2 Press .... **Shift** + **F9**

Calculate All Open Workbooks (When Calculation is Set to Manual)

Also updates all charts in open workbooks and calculates data tables when Calculation is set to Automatic Except Tables.

• Press **F9**

Replace All or Part of a Formula with Resulting Value

Permanently replaces the formula or part of the formula with its result.

1 Double-click .... ***cell containing formula to convert***

To replace part of a formula with its result:
   • Select .... ***part of formula to convert***

2 Press **F9**

3 Enter .... **⏎**
to replace formula with its result.

OR

Press .... **Esc**
to cancel.

Replace More than One Formula or an Array with Resulting Values

1 Select . . . . *cells containing formulas or entire array*

2 Click . . . . **Edit, Copy**

3 Click . . . . **Edit, Paste Special...**

4 Select . . . . ○ **Values**

5 Click . . . . `OK`

6 Press . . . . `ESC`
to end procedure.

Create a Link between Workbooks

1 Open . . . . *workbooks to link*

2 Arrange . . . . *workspace*
so both workbooks are in view.

3 Select . . . . *worksheet in source workbook*
containing cells to reference.

4 Select . . . . *cell(s) to reference*

5 Click . . . . **Edit, Copy**

6 Select . . . . *worksheet in dependent workbook*

7 Select . . . . *cell(s) to receive link*
NOTE: If referencing more than one cell,
select upper left cell in destination cell range.

To paste link as values:

a Click . . . . **Edit, Paste Special...**

b Click . . . . `Paste Link`
If a reference includes more than one cell, Excel creates a
single array formula in destination cells.

To paste link as a picture:

• Press Shift and click . . . . . . **Edit, Paste Picture Link**

8 Press . . . . `ESC`
to end procedure.

Type an External Reference in a Formula

*(Also see **Insert an External Reference in a Formula by Selecting It**, page 92.)*

In an external reference, special characters are used as follows:

- **Single quotation (')** – *encloses the path, filename and sheet-level name.*
- **Square brackets ([ ])** – *encloses the workbook filename.*
- **Exclamation signs (!)** – *separates the sheet name from the cell reference.*

1 If necessary, type or edit . . . . **formula**
*(See **Type New Formula**, page 79, and **Enable Cell Editing**, page 53.)*

2 Place . . . . **insertion point in formula**
where reference will be inserted.
NOTE: If necessary, type preceding operator or left parenthesis [(].

3 Press . . . . `'`

4 Type . . . . **path to workbook file**

5 Press . . . . `[`

6 Type . . . . **workbook filename**

7 Press . . . . `]`

8 Type . . . . **worksheet name**

9 Press . . . . `'`

10 Press . . . . `!`

11 Type . . . . **cell reference**
NOTE: You can type a named reference.

EXAMPLE: `'c:\excel\[sales.xls]sheet2'!$A$1`

Insert an External Reference in a Formula by Selecting It

1 Open .... **workbooks to link**

2 Arrange .... **workspace**
so that both workbooks are in view.

3 Select .... **worksheet to receive formula**
in dependent workbook.

4 If necessary, type or edit .... **formula**
(See **Type New Formula**, *page 79, and* **Enable Cell Editing**, *page 53.)*

5 Place .... **insertion point in formula**
where reference will be inserted.
NOTE: If necessary, type preceding operator or left parenthesis [(].

6 Select .... **worksheet containing cells to reference**
in source workbook.

7 Select .... **cell(s) to reference**
in source worksheet.
Excel adds external reference to formula.

8 Type or build .... **other formula parts**
OR
Enter .... ⏎

Remove Links between Workbooks

(See **Replace All or Part of a Formula with Resulting Value**, *page 89,
and* **Replace More than One Formula or an Array with Resulting Values**,
page 90.)

Manage Links (from Dependent Workbook)

1 Open or select . . . . *dependent workbook*

2 Click . . . . **Edit, Links...**
Excel lists all source workbooks for the dependent workbook.

To exit dialog and return to dependent workbook:

• Click . . . . Close

To update values from source files:

a Select source file(s) . . . . **Source File** list

b Click . . . . Update Now

To open source files:

a Select source file(s) . . . . **Source File** list

b Click . . . . Open

To replace the source with another workbook:

a Select source file to replace in . . . . **Source File** list

b Click . . . . Change Source...

c Select new source file in . . . . **File Name** list

d Click . . . . OK

Save Linked Workbooks

NOTE: *Saving the source workbook(s) prior to saving the dependent workbook ensures that the workbook names in the external references are current.*

1 Select and save . . . . *source workbook(s)*
supplying the linked references.

2 Select and save . . . . *dependent workbook*
that received linked references.
*(See **Save Active Workbook As**, page 31, and **Save Previously Saved Active Workbook**, page 31.)*

Create a One-Input Data Table

NOTE: *An illustrated example with labeled items follows these steps.*

1   Enter (item A) . . . . ***initial value in input cell***

2   Enter (item B) . . . . ***series of substitution values***
in desired column or row.

3   Select . . . . ***cell to receive formula***

If substitution values are in a <u>column</u>,

- Select (item C) . . . . . ***cell one position above and right***
of first substitution value.

If substitution values are in a <u>row</u>,

- Select . . . . ***cell one position below and left***
of first substitution value.

4   Enter (item C) . . . . ***formula that refers to input cell***

5   Select (item D) . . . . ***data table range***
containing formula, substitution values, and cells
where results will be displayed.

6   Click . . . . **Data, Table...**

7   Specify reference to input cell:

If substitution values are in a <u>row</u>,

- Select (in worksheet) or type reference
to initial input cell in . . . . **Row Input Cell:** [   ]

If substitution values are in a <u>column</u>,

- Select (in worksheet) or type reference (item A)
to initial input cell in . . . . . **Column Input Cell:** [   ]

8   Click . . . . [OK]

Continued ...

Create a One-Input Data Table (continued)

Example of one-input data table:

Create a Two-Input Data Table

NOTE: An illustrated example with labeled items follows these steps.

1   Enter (Item A) . . . . **initial value in row input cell**

2   Enter (item B) . . . . **initial value in column input cell**

3   Enter (item C) . . **series of substitution values in a column**

4   Enter (item C) . . . . . **series of substitution values in a row**
   NOTE: The first value in row and column are shared.

5   Select (item D) . **cell containing shared substitution value**

6   Enter . . . . **formula**
   NOTE: Formula must refer to row (item A)
   and column (item B) input cells.

7   Select (item E) . . . . **data table range**
   containing formula, substitution values, and
   cells where results will be displayed.

8   Click . . . . **Data, Table...**

9   Select (in worksheet) or type reference (item A)
   to row input cell in . . . . **Row Input Cell:** [   ]

Continued ...

Create a Two-Input Data Table (continued)

10 Select (in worksheet) or type reference (item B)
to column input cell in . . . . . . **Column Input Cell:** [   ]

11 Click . . . . [OK]

Example of two-input data table:

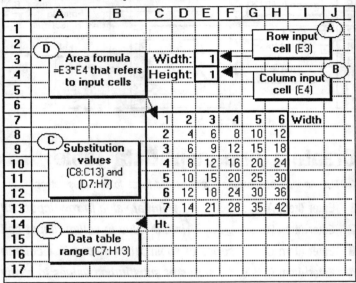

A Row input cell (E3)

B Column input cell (E4)

D Area formula =E3*E4 that refers to input cells

Width: 1
Height: 1

C Substitution values (C8:C13) and (D7:H7)

	1	2	3	4	5	6	Width
2	4	6	8	10	12	
3	6	9	12	15	18	
4	8	12	16	20	24	
5	10	15	20	25	30	
6	12	18	24	30	36	
7	14	21	28	35	42	

Ht.

E Data table range (C7:H13)

Add Substitution Input Values to a Data Table

1 Type . . *new substitution values in cells adjacent to table*

2 Select . . . . *entire data table range*
<u>and</u> extend . . . . *selection*
to include new cells.

3 Follow steps **6-8** to create a one-input table, page 94.

  OR

  Follow steps **8-11** to create a two-input table, pages 95 and 96.

Select an Entire Data Table or Array

1 Select . . . . *any result cell in data table or array*
2 Press . . . . Ctrl + /

Clear an Entire Data Table or Array

1 Select . . . . *any result cell in data table or array*
2 Press . . . . Ctrl + /
to select entire range.
3 Press . . . . Del
OR
  a Right-click . . . . *any selected cell in range*
  b Click . . . . **Clear Contents**

Clear Results in a Data Table or Array

1 Select . *all cells containing results in data table or array*
2 Press . . . . Del
OR
  a Right-click . . . . *any selected cell in range*
  b Click . . . . **Clear Contents**

Create a Lookup Table

Finds information located in a table:
- *VLOOKUP — compares values listed in a column.*
- *HLOOKUP — compares values listed in a row.*

NOTE: *An illustrated example with labeled items for VLOOKUP follows these steps.*

1 Enter (item A) . . . . . . ***compare values in a column or row***

2 Enter (item B) . . ***data in cells adjacent to compare values***

3 Enter (item C) . . . . ***an initial compare value to find***

4 Select (item D). . . . ***cell where result of lookup will appear***

5 Press . . . . 🔳

6 Type function name . . . . **VLOOKUP** or **HLOOKUP**

7 Press . . . . 🔳

8 Select (in worksheet)
or type (item C) ***reference containing compare value to find***

9 Press . . . . 🔳

10 Select (in worksheet)
or type (item E) . . . . ***reference to entire lookup area***

11 Press . . . . 🔳

12 Type . . . . ***offset number***
representing the column offset (for VLOOKUP) or row
offset (for HLOOKUP) in table where data is located.
EXAMPLE: Type a 2 if you want to show data located in second column of table.

13 Press . . . . 🔳

14 Click . . . . ☐ OK

Continued ...

Calculate

99

Create a Lookup Table (continued)

Example of Vlookup table:

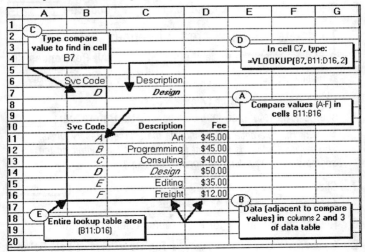

Consolidate Data by Category

Consolidates data not positioned in the same cells on their respective worksheets. Data in source areas that has identical labels will be grouped together and summarized in the destination worksheet.

If data to consolidate is in separate workbooks,

- Open and arrange . . . . **workbooks**

1 Make sure category labels of data to group are identical and consistently placed above or to the left of data.

2 Select . . . . **destination worksheet**

If destination worksheet contains outlining,

- Clear (page 133) . . . . **outline**

3 Select . . . . **upper left cell**
in area to receive consolidated data.
*NOTE: This cell can be on a separate worksheet
or on the same worksheet as the source data.*

Continued ...

Consolidate Data by Category (continued)

4 Click . . . . **Data, Consolidate...**

5 Select desired summary function in . . . . **Function** [⬇]

To delete a source area reference:

a Select reference to delete in . . . . **All References** list

b Click . . . . [**Delete**]

6 Select (in worksheet) or type
source area reference in . . . . **Reference:** [   ]
*NOTE: The reference should include the source category labels.
The easiest method is to select the worksheet tab containing the
source data, then select the appropriate cell(s).*

7 Click . . . . [**Add**]
Excel enters reference in All References list.

8 Repeat steps **6** and **7** for each source reference to add.

9 Select . . . . ☐ **Top Row** or ☐ **Left Column**
NOTE: Excel will then use the labels to consolidate by category.

To ensure consolidated data remains current:

• Select . . . . ☐ **Create Links to Source Data**
*NOTE: You cannot link the data if the destination range is on the
same worksheet as the source data.*

10 Click . . . . [**OK**]

Consolidate Data by Position

Consolidates similar categories of data positioned in the same cells on their respective worksheets.

If data to consolidate is in separate workbooks,

- Open and arrange . . . . *workbooks*

1 Make sure data to consolidate in source areas is arranged in the same absolute positions on their respective worksheets.

2 Select . . . . *destination worksheet*

If destination worksheet contains outlining,

- Clear (page 133) . . . . *outline*

3 Select . . . . *range to receive consolidated data*
   NOTE: *If you typed category labels, do not include them in selection. This range can be on a separate worksheet or on the same worksheet as the source data.*

4 Click . . . . **Data, Consolidate...**

5 Select desired summary function in . . . . **Function** ⬚⬚⬚ 🔽

To delete a source area reference:

   a Select reference to delete in . . . . **All References** list

   b Click . . . . `Delete`

6 Select (in worksheet) or type
   source area reference in . . . . **Reference:** ⬚⬚⬚
   NOTE: *The easiest method is to select the worksheet tab containing the source data, then select the appropriate cell(s).*

7 Click . . . . `Add`
   Excel enters reference in All References list.

8 Repeat steps **6** and **7** for each source reference to add.

To create a link to the source data:

- Select . . . . ☐ **Create Links to Source Data**
   NOTE: *You cannot link the data if the destination range is on the same worksheet as the source data.*

9 Click . . . . `OK`

Create an Array Formula

NOTE: An illustrated example with labeled items is provided below.

1 Type (item A) . . . . *values to be calculated*
by array formula in consecutive cells.

2 Select (item B) . . . *range of cells to receive array formula*
(the cells where results will appear).

3 Type (item C) . . . . *formula*
*NOTE: In the formula, be sure to specify entire range of
cells containing values to calculate (such as the values 1 through 6 in
the example).*

4 Press . . . . **Ctrl** + **Shift** + **←┘**
*Excel adds braces ({ }) to formula and displays resulting values in each
cell in array selection area (item B).*

Example of an Array Formula:

	A	B	C	D	E	F	G	
1								
2								
3			POINT/INCH CONVERSION TABLE					
4								
5						Type formula		
6			PTS	INCHES		=C7:C12/72		
7		Values	1	0.013889				
8		calculated by	2	0.027778		then press		
9		array formula	3	0.041667		CTRL+SHIFT+ENTER		
10		(C7:C12)	4	0.055556		(to create array formula)		
11			5	0.069444				
12			6	0.083333		Array		
13						selection area		
14						(D7:D12) will		
15						display results		
16								
17								

A — Values calculated by array formula (C7:C12)

C — Type formula =C7:C12/72 then press CTRL+SHIFT+ENTER (to create array formula)

B — Array selection area (D7:D12) will display results

Edit an Array Formula

1 Double-click . . . . *any result cell in array*
2 Edit . . . . *formula as desired*
3 Press . . . . `Ctrl` + `Shift` + `↵`
Excel changes all formulas in array.

Extend an Array Formula to Include Additional Cells

1 Enter . . . . *new values for array formula*
to calculate in cells adjacent to existing array data.
2 Select . . . . *all cells in array*
<u>and</u> extend . . . . *selection*
to include new cells where results will appear.
3 Double-click . . . . *any result cell in array*
4 Edit . . . . *formula as desired*
NOTE: *In the formula, be sure to include reference
to cells containing new values to calculate.*
5 Press . . . . `Ctrl` + `Shift` + `↵`

Enter an Array Constant in an Array Formula

NOTE: *Use an array constant to specify multiple values in an array formula
instead of referring to values contained in the worksheet.*

1 Select . . . . *first cell to receive array formula*
<u>and</u> extend . . . . *selection*
to include cells in which results will appear.
2 Type . . . . *formula*
3 Place . . . . *insertion point*
where array constant will be inserted.
4 Type . . . . *array constant*
in one of the following ways:

Continued ...

Enter an Array Constant in an Array Formula (continued)

To type an array constant when results will appear in a single row:

a Press . . . . 【

b Type . . . . *numbers to calculate in #,#,# format*

c Press . . . . 】
  Formula example: ={1,2,3,4}*2
  Result of example: 2 4 6 8

To type an array constant when results will appear in a single column:

a Press . . . . 【

b Type . . . . *numbers to calculate in #;#;# format*

c Press . . . . 】
  Formula example: ={2;3;4}*2
  Result of example: 4
                          6
                          8

To type an array constant when results will appear in a row and column:

a Press . . . . 【

b Type . . *numbers to calculate in #,#,#;#,#,# format*

c Press . . . . 】
  Formula example: ={1,2;3,4}*2
  Result of example: 2 4
                       6 8
  NOTE: *Commas separate values in same row.*
  Semicolons separate rows.

5 Complete formula, then press . . . . **Ctrl** + **Shift** + **↵**

Find a Specific Solution to a Formula (Goal Seek)

1 Enter . . . . *formula and dependent values*

2 Click . . . . **Tools, Goal Seek...**

3 Select (cell in worksheet) or type
reference to cell containing formula in . . . . **Set cell:** [ ]

4 Type desired formula result value in . . . . **To value:** [ ]

5 Select (cell in worksheet) or type reference to cell
containing value to change in . . . **By changing cell:** [ ]

6 Click . . . . [OK]
Excel displays status of goal seeking.

7 If desired, select . . . . **Goal Seek Status options:**
Pause, Step, Continue

8 Click . . . . [OK]
to replace value in worksheet with solution value.
OR
Click . . . . [Cancel]
to retain original values.

Use Solver to Find the Best Answer

1 Enter . . . . *formula and dependent values*

2 Click . . . . **Tools, Solver...**
NOTE: *If Solver is not on the Tools menu,
see **Install or Remove an Add-In**, page 173.*

3 Select (in worksheet) or type
reference to target cell in . . . . . . **Set Target Cell:** [ ]
NOTE: *Target cell typically contains a formula referring to cells
that will change. If target cell is not a formula, it must also be
included as a changing cell (step 4).*

4 Select (in worksheet) or type
references to changing cells in . **By Changing Cells:** [ ]
NOTES: *Type commas between references to non-adjacent cells.
Click the Guess button to have Solver propose changing cells.*
Continued ...

Use Solver to Find the Best Answer (continued)

To solve for a specific value:

a Select .... ○ **Value of**

b Type target value in .... **Value of:** [   ]

To solve for a maximum or minimum target value:
(Requires you to set constraints)

• Select .... ○ **Max** or ○ **Min**

To add constraints:

a Click .... [Add...]

b Select (in worksheet) or type <u>reference</u> to
cell to apply constraint to ... **Cell Reference:** [   ]

c Select constraint operator in .... **Constraint:** [⬧]

d Specify constraint value in ...... **Constraint:** [   ]
*NOTE: You can select (in worksheet) a reference in a
cell containing the value or type a value or reference.*

To add another constraint:

1. Click .... [Add]
2. Repeat steps **b-d**, as needed.

e Click .... [OK]

To <u>change</u> a constraint:

a Select constraint in ..... **Subject to the Constraints** list

b Click .... [Change...]

c Edit .... *constraint elements*

d Click .... [OK]

To <u>delete</u> a constraint:

a Select constraint in ..... **Subject to the Constraints** list

b Click .... [Delete]

Continued ...

Use Solver to Find the Best Answer (continued)

To set **advanced** options:

a Click .... | Options... |

b Select .... ***Solver options:***

Max Time – limits time taken by Solver to find a solution.
Iterations – limits number of iterations used to find a solution.
Precision – sets precision for solutions.
Tolerance – sets percentage of error allowed in a solution.
Assume Linear Model – select to speed process in linear models.
Show Iteration Results – select to display results of each iteration.
Use Automatic Scaling – select to speed process when input and
     output values differ by large degrees.
Estimates (Tangent, Quadratic) – sets estimate process method.
Derivatives (Forward, Central) – sets derivative process method.
Search (Newton, Conjugate) – sets search direction for iterations.
Load Model... – loads model settings saved with Save Model
command.
Save Model... – saves current model setting in worksheet.

c Click .... | OK |

5 Click .... | Solve |

To create report(s) on a separate worksheet(s):

• Select report type(s) in .... **Reports** list

To save problem for use with Scenario Manager:

a Click .... | Save Scenario... |

b Type scenario name in ...... **Scenario Name:** [   ]

c Click .... | OK |

6 Select .... ◯ **Keep Solver Solution**
OR
Select .... ◯ **Restore Original Values**
NOTE: *You can restore original values and still generate selected
reports showing solutions.*

7 Click .... | OK |
to accept selected options.
OR
Click .... | Cancel |
to ignore settings and retain original values.

Create a Scenario

Scenarios are named sets of input values that quickly show different results in specified changing cells. There can be only one set of changing cells in a worksheet.

1 Enter . . . . *formula and initial values*

2 Click . . . . **Tools, Scenarios...**

   NOTE: *If Scenarios is not on the Tools menu,
   see* **Install or Remove an Add-In,** *page 173.*

3 Click . . . . [**Add...**]

4 Type name for scenario in . . . . . . **Scenario Name:** [   ]

5 Select (in worksheet) or type
   references of changing cells in . . . **Changing Cells:** [   ]

To edit comment:

* Edit text in . . . . **Comment** list

To set scenario protection options:

* Select or deselect . . . . **Protection options:**
   Prevent Changes — select to prevent others from making changes to
      scenario. (When Worksheet Protection is turned on.)
   Hide — select to prevent scenario name from being displayed in
      Scenario Manager dialog box. (When Worksheet Protection is
      turned on.)

6 Click . . . . [**OK**]

7 Type values in . . . . *each changing cell's* [   ]

To add scenario and create another scenario:

   a Click . . . . [**Add**]

   b Repeat steps **4-7**, as needed.

8 Click . . . . [**OK**]

9 Select scenario to show in . . . . **Scenarios** list

10 Click . . . . [**Show**]

11 If desired, repeat steps **9** and **10**.

12 Click . . . . [**Close**]

Use and Manage Scenarios

1 Click .... **Tools**, **Scenarios...**

To show a scenario:
a Select scenario to show in .... **Scenarios** list
b Click .... `Show`

To edit a scenario:
a Select scenario to edit in .... **Scenarios** list
b Click .... `Edit...`
c Follow steps 4-8 for **Create a Scenario**, page 108.

To delete a scenario:
a Select scenario to delete in .... **Scenarios** list
b Click .... `Delete`

To merge scenarios:
a Click .... `Merge...`
b Select workbook name
containing saved scenario in .... **Book:** `□`
c Select sheet containing scenarios
to merge in .... **Sheet** list
d Click .... `OK`

To create scenario report on separate worksheet:
a Click .... `Summary...`
b Select .... ○ **Scenario Summary**
OR
Select .... ○ **Scenario PivotTable**
If Scenario PivotTable,
  • Select (in worksheet) or type
  references to results cells in .. **Result Cells:** `□`
  NOTE: If you type references to non-adjacent cells, type commas between each reference.

c Click .... `OK`
2 Click .... `OK`

110

Pivot Tables

Create a Pivot Table

A pivot table is an interactive tool used to analyze information about worksheet data. For example, if you have a list containing information about expenses, a pivot table could evaluate the categories of these expenses, as shown in the illustration.

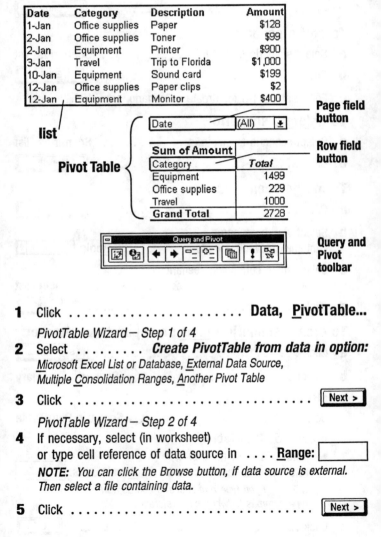

1 Click . . . . **Data, PivotTable...**

PivotTable Wizard – Step 1 of 4

2 Select . . . . **Create PivotTable from data in option:**
Microsoft Excel List or Database, External Data Source,
Multiple Consolidation Ranges, Another Pivot Table

3 Click . . . . `Next >`

PivotTable Wizard – Step 2 of 4

4 If necessary, select (in worksheet)
or type cell reference of data source in . . . . **Range:** ☐
NOTE: *You can click the Browse button, if data source is external. Then select a file containing data.*

5 Click . . . . `Next >`

Continued ...

Create a Pivot Table (continued)

PivotTable Wizard – Step 3 of 4

6 Create . . . . **pivot table layout**

To add fields to pivot table:

- Drag . . . . **field buttons**
  onto . . . . **a layout area**
  PAGE area – *to display specific page items in table.*
  ROW area – *to create row labels for each unique item in field.*
  COLUMN area – *to create column labels for each unique item in field.*
  DATA area – *to specify field to summarize.*
  NOTE: *You must include at least one field in the Data area.*
  You can drag more than one field button into a layout area,
  but it best to limit the number of fields when starting out.

To remove a field from pivot table:

- Drag . . . . **field button off the layout area**

To move a field to another layout area:

- Drag . . . . **field button onto desired layout area**

To modify how the field is used:

a Double-click . . . . **field button in layout area**

b Select (page 113, step 2) . . . . . **PivotTable Field options**

7 Click . . . . `Next >`

PivotTable Wizard – Step 4 of 4

8 Select (in worksheet) or type reference to upper-left
   destination of table in . . . **PivotTable Starting Cell:** [   ]
   NOTE: *if you leave this blank, Excel will create the pivot table on a*
   new worksheet. Do not place the pivot table where it can overwrite
   existing data.

9 If desired, type name in . . . . . . **PivotTable Name:** [   ]

10 Select . . . . **PivotTable options:**
   Grand Totals For Columns, Grand Totals For Rows,
   Save Data With Table Layout, AutoFormat Table

11 Click . . . . `Finish`

Excel displays pivot table, and the Query and Pivot toolbar appears.

Modify a Pivot Table

1 Select . . . . *any cell in pivot table*

2 Click . . . . *PivotTable Wizard button* 🗊
on Query and Pivot toolbar.

OR

Click . . . . **Data, PivotTable...**

3 If desired, make changes . . . . *to field layout*

AND/OR

Click . . . . `Next >` or `< Back`

To change:	PivotTable Wizard	Page
Data source	Step 1	110
Reference to source data	Step 2	110
Fields in layout	Step 3	111
Pivot table position, Pivot table name	Step 4	111

   Summary options – Grand Totals For Columns, Grand Totals For Rows,
   Save Data With Table Layout, AutoFormat Table.

4 Click . . . . `Finish`

Update a Pivot Table

Updates a pivot table to show changes made to source data.
NOTE: *If rows or columns were removed or added to the source data
range, you may have to follow the steps to modify a pivot table (page 112)
and change the reference to the source data.*

1 Select . . . . *any cell in pivot table*

2 Click . . . . *Refresh Data button* ❗
on Query and Pivot toolbar.

OR

Click . . . . **Data, Refresh Data**

Modify a Pivot Table Field

Specifies how the pivot table will display or process the field data.

1 Double-click . . . . **desired field button in pivot table**

OR

Click . . . . **PivotTable Field button** 🔁
on Query and Pivot toolbar.

OR

From PivotTable Wizard – Step 3 of 4
Double-click . . . . **desired field button in layout area**

2 Select . . . . **PivotTable Field options:**

Data field options *(from PivotTable Wizard only):*
Na_me – to change field name.
Summarize by – Sum, Count, Average, Max, Min, Product, Count Nums,
     StdDev, StdDevp, Var, Varp.
Number... – to format values in data field.
Options >> – to specify a custom calculation to show data as: Normal,
     Difference From, % Of, % Difference From, Running Total in,
     % of row, % of column, % of total, Index.
Delete – to delete field from pivot table.

Row, Column, or Page field options:
Name – to change field name.
Orientation – to change orientation of field to Row, Column, or Page.
Hide Items – to select/deselect items to hide for field.
Delete – to delete field from pivot table.
Subtotals – Automatic, Custom, or None.
          If Custom, select Sum, Count, Average, Max, Min,
          Product, Count Nums, StdDev, StdDevp, Var, Varp.

3 Click . . . . ⟦ OK ⟧

Move or Remove Fields on a Pivot Table (by Dragging)

- Drag .... **field button**
  onto .... **desired area in or off pivot table**

  NOTE: *Pointer indicates the result of the move as follows:*

  - *Move field to column* .... ⬚
  - *Move field to row* .... ⬚
  - *Move field to page* .... ⬚
  - *Remove field from pivot table* .... ✖

Move Field Items in a Pivot Table

Changes position of an item and its related data within a field.
NOTE: *You can also sort (page 118) items in row or column fields.*

1 Select .... **cell containing item**

2 Point to .... **border of cell**
  Pointer becomes a ↖.

3 Drag .... **border outline to desired position in field**
  NOTE: *Excel will restrict movement to the field.*

Create a Group Field for Items in a Pivot Table

Groups items in fields to create a new field category containing the items you select. For example, you might group office supplies and equipment expense items to find totals for these items.

1 Select .... **items in a field(s) to combine**
  NOTE: *Selected items do not have to be adjacent.*

2 Click .... **Group button** [→]
  on Query and Pivot toolbar.

  Excel creates a new field containing the grouped items.

Remove a Group Field in a Pivot Table

1 Select .... *any cell in grouped field*
2 Click .... *Ungroup button* ⟵
on Query and Pivot toolbar.

Modify a Group Field in a Pivot Table

(See Modify a Pivot Table Field, page 113.)

Group Date, Time, or Numeric Items in a Pivot Table Field

1 Select .... *cell containing value to group*
2 Click .... *Group button* ⟶
on Query and Pivot toolbar.

To change proposed start and end for group:

- Type values in .... **S**tarting at and **E**nding at [   ]

To change proposed interval for group:

- Select (for time or date) or
type (for numbers) an interval in .... **B**y list

  If Days,

  - Select or type number
  of days in .... **N**umber of Days: [⇕]

3 Click .... [OK]

Undo Last Change to Pivot Table

- Click .... **E**dit, **U**ndo Pivot

Hide Details in a Pivot Table

NOTE: *You can double-click a field <u>item</u> to hide its details. Be careful not to double-click a data field item, doing so will create a worksheet that displays data for the item.*

1 Click . . . . ***an item in a field***
to hide subordinate data for item.

OR

Click . . . . ***a field button***
to hide all subordinate data for the field.

2 Click . . . . ***Hide Detail button*** ⊟
on Query and Pivot toolbar.

OR

Click . . . . . <u>**D**</u>ata, <u>**G**</u>roup and Outline ▸, <u>**H**</u>ide Detail

Show Hidden Details in a Pivot Table

NOTE: *You can also double-click a field <u>item</u> to show its details. Be careful not to double-click a data field item, doing so will create a worksheet that displays data for the item.*

1 Click . . . . ***item***
to show hidden data for item.

OR

Click . . . . ***a field button***
to show all hidden data for the field.

2 Click . . . . ***Show Detail button*** ⊞
on Query and Pivot toolbar.

OR

Click . . . . <u>**D**</u>ata, <u>**G**</u>roup and Outline ▸, <u>**S**</u>how Detail

If no hidden details exist for field or item,

FROM SHOW DETAIL DIALOG BOX

• Double-click . . . . ***desired field name to show***

Display Specific Page Items in a Pivot Table

- Select item in .... *page field's* [_____ ⬇]

Display All Page Items in a Pivot Table

- Select (All) in .... *page field's* [_____ ⬇]

Create a Worksheet for each Page Field Item in a Pivot Table

Creates separate worksheets displaying data for each item in a Page field.

1 Select .... *any cell in pivot table*

2 Click .... *Show Pages Button* 🖽
on Query and Pivot toolbar.

3 Select page field in .... **Show All Pages of** list

4 Click .... [OK]

Create a Worksheet for a Specific Page Field Item in a Pivot Table

- Double-click .... *data field item*
for desired page item.

Sort Pivot Table Data

1 Select . . . . *any item in field to sort*

2 Click . . . . **Data, Sort...**

To change proposed sort by cell:

- Select (in worksheet) or
  type reference to cell in . . . . **Sort by:** [　　]

To set the sort order:

- Select . . . . ○ **Ascending** or ○ **Descending**

To sort by values or alphabetically:

- Select . . . . ○ **Values** or ○ **Labels**
  *NOTE: To select Values, the **sort by** reference (see above)
  must contain a value in the data area of the pivot table.*

To select a custom sort order
(i.e., days or months):

a Click . . . . [Options...]

b Select desired order in . . **First Key Sort Order** [　　▼]

c Click . . . . [OK]

3 Click . . . . [OK]

Sort Data

1 Select . . . . *any cell in list*

OR

Select . . . . *range of cells to sort*

2 Click . . . . **Data, Sort...**

To change orientation of sort (columns to rows):

a Click . . . . `Options...`

b Select . . . . ◯ **Sort Left to Right**

c Click . . . . `OK`

To set the first key sort order:

a Select column or row in . . . . **Sort By:** `▯`

b Select . . . . ◯ **Ascending** or ◯ **Descending**

To set additional key sort orders:

a Select column or row in . . . . **Then By:** `▯`

b Select . . . . ◯ **Ascending** or ◯ **Descending**

To select a custom sort order first key:

a Click . . . . `Options...`

b Select desired order in . . **First Key Sort Order** `▯`

c Click . . . . `OK`

To specify a case sensitive sort order:

a Click . . . . `Options...`

b Select . . . . ☐ **Case Sensitive**

c Click . . . . `OK`

To include or exclude header row from sort:

• Select . . . . ◯ **No Header Row** or ◯ **Header Row**

Continued ...

Sort Data (continued)

To specify a case sensitive sort order:

a Click .... | Options... |

b Select .... ☐ **Case Sensitive**

c Click .... | OK |

3 Click .... | OK |

NOTES: To sort by more than three columns, sort the list using the least important columns. Then, repeat the sort using the most important columns.

When you sort rows that are part of an outline, Excel will keep outline families together. When you sort rows containing graphics, Excel will move the graphics with rows, if the graphics are set to move with the cell (page 184).

Perform a Quick Sort

1 Select .... *cell in list to sort by*
NOTE: Excel will apply setting made in a previous sort, if one was made.

OR

Select .... *range of cells to sort*
NOTE: The active cell in the range determines the column Excel will sort by.

OR

Select .... *item in pivot table field to sort by*

2 Click .... *Sort Ascending button* [A↓Z]

OR

Click .... *Sort Descending button* [Z↓A]
on Standard toolbar.

Undo a Sort

NOTE: To successfully undo a sort, you must undo it immediately.

• Click .... **Edit, Undo Sort**

Repeat a Sort

1 Select .... *cell(s) to sort*
2 Click .... **Edit, Repeat Sort**

Create or Edit Custom Lists

You can use a custom list to fill cells with a series and as a custom sort order.

1 Click .... **Tools, Options...**
2 Click .... | Custom Lists |

To create a custom list:

a Select NEW LIST in .... **Custom Lists** list
b Type list items in .... **List Entries** list
   NOTE: Items cannot begin with a number.
   Enter items in the order you want Excel to use
   when creating a series or sorting a list.

c Click .... | Add |

To import a custom list from worksheet:

a Select (in worksheet) or type
   reference to cells
   containing list items in ...**Import List from Cells:** | |
b Click .... | Import |

To edit a created custom list:

a Select list to edit in .... **Custom Lists** list
b Edit list items in .... **List Entries** list

To delete a created custom list:

a Select list to delete in .... **Custom Lists** list
b Click .... | Delete |
c Click .... | OK |
3 Click .... | OK |

Lists

Excel automatically recognizes a labeled series of rows containing sets of data as a list. In a list, Excel treats rows as records and columns as fields. The field names are derived from the column labels.

Add Records to a List (Using a Data Form)

1 Select .... *any cell in list*

2 Click .... <u>D</u>ata, F<u>o</u>rm...

3 Click .... New

4 Type data in each .... *record field* [_____]

*NOTE: Press **Tab** to move to next field. Do not press **Enter** after typing data in field, unless you want to add another record.*

To add additional records:

• Repeat steps **3** and **4** for each record to add.

5 Click .... Close

Delete Records from a List (Using a Data Form)

Caution: Deleted records cannot be restored.

1 Select .... *any cell in list*

2 Click .... <u>D</u>ata, F<u>o</u>rm...

3 Display (page 123) .... *record to delete*

4 Click .... Delete

5 Click .... OK

To delete additional records:

• Repeat steps **3-5** for each record to delete.

6 Click .... Close

Excel deletes record in list, and moves records up to close the space left by the deletion.

Display or Edit Records (Using a Data Form)

1 Select . . . . *any cell in list*

2 Click . . . . **D**ata, F**o**rm...

To view next record:

- Click . . . . *down scroll arrow* ⊞ or ⸤ Find **N**ext ⸥

To view previous record:

- Click . . . . *up scroll arrow* ⊞ or ⸤ Find **P**rev ⸥

To scroll to a record:

- Drag . . . . *scroll box* ☐

To move forward ten records:

- Click . . . . *below scroll box*

To move back ten records:

- Click . . . . *above scroll box*

To edit displayed record:

- Edit data in each . . . . *record field* ⸤_____⸥
  to change.
  NOTE: *Do not press* **Enter** *after typing data in field.*

To cancel changes made to current record:

- Click . . . . ⸤ **R**estore ⸥
  NOTE: *You must restore before moving to another record.*

3 Click . . . . ⸤ C**l**ose ⸥

Find Specific Records
(Using a Data Form)

1 Select .... *any cell in list*

2 Click .... <u>D</u>ata, F<u>o</u>rm...

3 Click .... | Criteria |

4 Type a criterion for which to search in.. *record field* | |

NOTE: Wildcard characters (? or *) may be used to stand for one (?) or more (*) characters in the position of the wildcard character. To find an actual ? or * , precede ? or * character with a tilde (~).

EXAMPLES:

> Type pau *in a text field to find records beginning with* pau, *such as* Paul *or* Paula.

> Type >=1/1/89 *in a date field to find records containing dates on or after* 1/1/89.

> Type (718) ???-???? *in a character field to find phone numbers that have a* 718 *area code.*

> Type * Shaw *in a character field to find records that have* **any** *first name and* Shaw *as a last name.*

5 To add criteria to additional fields, repeat step **4**.

6 Click .... | Find <u>N</u>ext |

   OR

   Click .... | Find <u>P</u>rev |

7 Repeat step **6** for each matching record to find.

To obtain access to entire list:

a Click .... | Criteria |

b Click .... | C<u>l</u>ear |

c Click .... | Cl<u>o</u>se |

8 Click .... | Cl<u>o</u>se |

   to return to worksheet.

Filter a List Automatically

NOTE: *You can use AutoFilter with one list in a worksheet at a time and the list must have column labels.*

1 Click .... ***any cell in list***

2 Click .... **Data, Filter ▸, AutoFilter**
Excel adds drop-down list arrows next to each column label.

3 Click .... ⬇
of label containing data to display.

4 Select .... ***item from list***
In addition to a specific item you can select:
- ***(All)*** — to show all items in the column.
- ***(Blank)*** — to show only records that have no data in the column.
- ***(NonBlanks)*** — to show only records that have data in the column.
- ***(Custom...)*** — to specify up to two comparison criteria for data in the column.

If Custom was selected,

a Select a column item in first .... [⬇]

b Select desired operator for item in .... [⬇]

To specify another criteria for column:

1. Select .... ○ **And** or ○ **Or**
2. Select column item in second .... [⬇]
3. Select desired operator for item in .... [⬇]

NOTE: *If you select criteria from more than one drop-down list, Excel will show only records meeting the criteria specified by both filters.*

End AutoFiltering

- Click .... **Data, Filter ▸, ✓AutoFilter**

Filter a List with Advanced Filtering

NOTE: *List must have column labels.*

1 Set up (pages 127 and 129) . . . . ***criteria range***

2 Select . . . . ***any cell in list***

3 Click . . . . **Data, Filter ▸, Advanced Filter...**

To change proposed list range:

• Select (in worksheet)
  or type range to filter in . . . . **List Range:** ⬚

4 Select (in worksheet)
  or type criteria range in . . . . **Criteria Range:** ⬚
  NOTE: *Include the comparison criteria column label(s) with the criteria.*

5 Select . . . . ◯ **Filter the List, in-place**

  OR

  a Select . . . . ◯ **Copy to Another Location**

  b Select (in worksheet) or
    type destination reference in . . . . **Copy to:** ⬚
    CAUTION: *If you indicate a single cell, Excel will copy the filtered results to cells below and to the right of the cell, overwriting existing data without warning.*

To hide duplicate records:

• Select . . . . ☐ **Unique Records Only**

6 Click . . . . | OK |

End In-Place Advanced Filtering

• Click . . . . **Data, Filter ▸, Show All**

Set Up a Criteria Range (for Comparison Criteria)

*Tells Excel how to filter a list, prior to using Advanced Filtering (page 126). For example, you might want Excel to display only records (rows) that meet either criterion: Region is **North** or Sales greater than or equal to **20000**.*

Region	January
North	
	>20000

Comparison criteria labels

Criteria range

Region	January	February
North	10111	13400
South	22100	24050
East	13270	15670
West	10800	21500

List range

Region	January	February
North	10111	13400
South	22100	24050

Results copied to another location

1 If necessary, insert . . . . *blank rows* above the list you want to filter.

2 Type or copy . . . . *desired column label(s)* to blank rows above list, as shown above.
*These labels are called **comparison criteria labels** and must be identical to the labels in the list you want to filter.*

GENERAL GUIDELINES FOR SETTING UP A CRITERIA RANGE:

- *Enter criteria below comparison criteria labels.*
- *The criteria range cannot contain empty columns.*
- *To show only records meeting all of the criteria in the criteria range, enter criteria in the same row.*
- *To show records meeting any of the criteria in the criteria range, enter criteria in different rows.*
- *To show records meeting different criteria for the same column, set up duplicate comparison criteria labels.*

3 Enter criteria . . . . *in row(s) below criteria labels*

Continued ...

Set Up a Criteria Range — For Comparison Criteria (continued)

To show only records (rows) matching a value, date, or text:

- Enter . . . . *text, number, date, or logical value* to find in column.

  EXAMPLE: Below **Region**, *type* **North**.

  NOTE: *When you enter text, Excel will find all items beginning with the text criteria. For example, if you enter* **Sam**, *Excel will include records such as* **Samuel** *and* **Sammy**.

Examples of criteria:

To find:	Examples
an exact text match	="=text to find"
any character in a specific position	Topic?
consecutive characters in a specific position	Sa*y
an actual question mark, asterisk, or tilde (~)	What is that~?
a value greater than a specified number	>1000

To show items that compare to a specified value:

- Use one of the following comparison operators before a value, date, or text criteria.

=	(equal to or matches)
>	(greater than)
<	(less than)
>=	(greater than or equal to)
<=	(less than or equal to)

  For example, enter >1000 *below the January comparison criteria label to show only records containing values greater than 1000 for that column.*

4 Filter (page 126) . . . . **list with Advanced Filtering** to show results of criteria.

Set Up a Criteria Range (for Computed Criteria)

Tells Excel how to filter a list based on a calculation, prior to using Advanced Filtering (page 126). The example below shows only records that have January sales greater than the average sales for February.

Criteria range {	Jan Sales		**Label for computed criteria**
	FALSE		**Formula** =C9>AVERAGE($D$9:$D$12) **evaluates to FALSE**

Region	January	February	**List range**
North	10111	13400	**(formula refers to**
South	22100	24050	**values in range**
East	13270	15670	**C9:D12)**
West	10800	21500	

Region	January	February	**Results copied**
South	22100	24050	**to another location**

1 If necessary, insert . . . . **blank rows** above list to filter.

2 Type . . . . **label(s) for computed criteria** in blank rows above list, as shown above.

*Important: These labels must **not** match column labels in the list to filter.*

GENERAL GUIDELINES FOR SETTING COMPUTED CRITERIA:

- *Enter criteria below labels for computed criteria.*
- *The criteria range cannot contain empty columns.*
- *To show only records meeting all of the criteria in the criteria range, enter criteria in the same row.*
- *To show records meeting any of the criteria in the criteria range, enter criteria in different rows.*
- *You can combine comparison (previous page) and calculated criteria to create complex conditions.*

3 Enter criteria formula in . . . . . **row(s) below labels for computed criteria**

GUIDELINES FOR CRITERIA FORMULA:

- *Use a relative reference to point to the first value in column you want to evaluate.*
- *Use an absolute reference to indicate the column you want to compare.*
- *The formula must produce a logical (TRUE or FALSE) value.*
- *The formula must refer to at least one column in the list.*

4 Filter (page 126) . . . . **list with Advanced Filtering**

Work with Lists Filtered In-Place

When a list is filtered:
- *One or more drop-down arrows change color.*
- *The status line reports the number of records (rows) found.*
- *The row headings change color.*

When you filter a list in-place, you can use the following commands to act on only the visible cells:

AutoFill, AutoSum, Chart, Clear, Copy, Delete, Format, Print, Sort, Subtotal

Functions Summarizing Values in Lists

Use the Function Wizard (page 80) to assist you in building the following functions as needed.

Total values in a range meeting a criteria

SUMIF(eval_range, "criteria", sum_range)

Count items in a range meeting a criteria

COUNTIF(eval_range, "criteria")

Count blank items in a range:

COUNTBLANK(eval_range)

Subtotal a List Automatically

Creates subtotals for groups of data in specified columns, and a grand total at the bottom of the list. Excel automatically applies outlining to the resulting list.

NOTE: *You can also do this to a filtered list.*

1 Sort (page 119) . . . . *column(s) in list to subtotal*
   NOTE: *List must contain labeled columns in its first row.*
   Items to subtotal should be grouped together.

2 Select . . . . *any cell in list*

3 Click . . . . **Data**, **Subtotals...**

4 Select column label containing
   groups to subtotal in . . . . . . **At Each Change in:** [＿＿＿＿＿ ±]

5 Select desired function in . . . . **Use Function:** [＿＿＿＿＿ ±]

6 Select column label(s) containing
   values to calculate in . . . . **Add Subtotal to** list

To replace or retain current subtotals:
- Select or deselect . . . . . . ☐ **Replace Current Subtotals**

To force page breaks between subtotaled groups:
- Select . . . . ☐ **Page Break Between Groups**

To place subtotals and grand totals above data:
- Deselect . . . . ☐ **Summary Below Data**

7 Click . . . . [OK]

Remove All Automatic Subtotals in a List

1 Select . . . . *any cell in subtotaled list*

2 Click . . . . **Data**, **Subtotals...**

3 Click . . . . [Remove All]

132

Lists

Create a Subtotal within a Subtotaled Group in a List

1 Sort (page 119) . . . . *columns in list to subtotal*

2 Subtotal (page 131) . . . . *first group in list*

3 Select . . . . *any cell in subtotaled list*

4 Click . . . . **Data, Subtotals...**

5 Select column label containing next group to subtotal in . . . **At Each Change in:** ⬜⬇

6 Select desired function in . . . . **Use Function:** ⬜⬇

7 Select column label(s) containing values to calculate in . . . . **Add Subtotals to** list

8 Deselect . . . . ⬜ **Replace Current Subtotals**

9 Click . . . . `OK`

Work with a Subtotaled List

Excel automatically applies outlining to the subtotaled list. You can use the outlining level buttons to hide or show the details you want. You can then print or chart the results, for example.

*(See **Show or Hide Outline Groups and Levels**, page 135.)*

Outline a Worksheet Automatically

NOTE: *In the data to outline, references in formulas must consistently point in one direction (i.e., summary formulas in rows must consistently refer to detail cells above them).*

1 Select . . . . *single cell to outline entire worksheet*

OR

Select . . . . *range of cells to outline*

2 Click . . . . **Data, Group and Outline ▸, Auto Outline**
Excel creates an outline and displays outline symbols to the left of the row heading and/or above column headings.

Clear Entire Outline

1 Select . . . . *and cell in outline*

2 Click . . . . **Data, Group and Outline ▸, Clear Outline**

Show or Hide Outline Symbols

1 Click . . . . **Tools, Options...**

2 Click . . . . | View |

3 Select or deselect . . . . ☐ **Outline Symbols**

4 Click . . . . | OK |

NOTE: *To quickly show or hide outline symbols, press Ctrl+8.*

Select an Outline Group (Using Outline Symbols)

1 If necessary, show (see above) . . . . *outline symbols*

2 Press **Shift** and click . . . . *show detail symbol* ⊞

OR

Press **Shift** and click . . . . *hide detail symbol* ⊟
of outline group to select.

Create or Change Outline Manually

1 Select . . . . *data to group*
NOTE: Select entire rows or columns containing detail data that is summarized by formulas below (for rows) or to the right (for columns).

OR

Select (page 133) . . . . *outline group to change*

2 Click . . . . **D**ata, **G**roup and Outline ▸

3 Click . . . . **G**roup...
to group data or demote level of selected group.

OR

Click . . . . **U**ngroup...
to ungroup or promote selected group.

If Group dialog box appears,

a Select . . . . ○ **R**ows or ○ **C**olumns

b Click . . . . [OK]
Excel displays outline symbols to the left of the row heading and/or above column headings.

4 Repeat steps **1-3** until you obtain desired outline structure.

Remove Group from Outline

1 Select (page 133) . . . . *group in outline to remove*

2 Click . . . . **D**ata, **G**roup and Outline ▸, **C**lear Outline

Show or Hide Outline Groups (Using Menu)

To show group details:

1 Select . . . . *summary data cell of group to expand*

2 Click . . . . **D**ata, **G**roup and Outline ▸, **S**how Detail

Continued ...

Show or Hide Outline Groups — Using Menu (continued)

To hide group details:

1 Select . . . . *summary data cell of group to collapse*

2 Click . . . . . **Data, Group and Outline ►, Hide Detail**

Show or Hide Outline Groups and Levels (Using Outline Symbols)

NOTE: *If outline symbols are not visible, see Show or Hide Outline Symbols, page 133.*

To show group details:

• Click . . . . *show detail symbol* ⊞
of group to expand.

To hide group details:

• Click . . . . *hide detail symbol* ⊟
of group to hide.

To show all outline groups for a level:

• Click . . . . *row or column level symbol*
for lowest level to show.

Select Only Visible Cells in Outline

Quickly formats, charts, moves or copies only the visible cells in an outline.

1 If necessary, hide groups or levels that are not to be selected (page 135).

2 Select . . . . *desired cells in outline*

3 Click . . . . **Edit, Go To...**

4 Click . . . . · Special...

5 Select . . . . ○ **Visible Cells Only**

6 Click . . . . OK

136

Change Column Widths

To change one column width:

1 Point to . . . . *right border of column heading*
Pointer becomes a ⟷.

2 Drag . . . . ⟷ *left or right*
Excel displays width on left side of formula bar.

To change several column widths:

1 Select . . . . *columns*
NOTE: *Click Select All button ⌷ to change all columns.*

2 Point to . . . . . *right border of any selected column heading*
Pointer becomes a ⟷.

3 Drag . . . . ⟷ *left or right*
Excel displays width on left side of formula bar.

To set column width to fit the longest entry:

• Double-click . . . . *right border of the column's heading*

To set column width to a specific size:

1 Select . . . . *any cell in column or columns to size*
2 Click . . . . **F̲ormat, C̲olumn** ▸, **W̲idth...**
3 Type number (0-255) in . . . . **C̲olumn Width:** ☐
NOTE: *Number represents number of characters that
can be displayed in cell using the standard font.*

4 Click . . . . ☐ OK ☐

Set Standard Column Width

*Changes column widths that have not been previously adjusted in selected
worksheet(s).*

1 Click . . . . **F̲ormat, C̲olumn** ▸, **Standard Width**
2 Type new number in . . . . . **Standard Column Width:** ☐
NOTE: *Number represents number of characters that
can be displayed in cell using the standard font.*

3 Click . . . . ☐ OK ☐

Reset Columns to the Standard Column Width

1 Select .... *column(s)*

2 Click .... **Format, Column** ▸, **Standard Width**

3 Click .... [OK]

Change Row Heights

To change one row height:

1 Point to .... *bottom border of row heading*
Pointer becomes a ↕.

2 Drag .... ↕ *up or down*
Excel displays height on left side of formula bar.

To change several row heights:

1 Select .... *rows*
NOTE: *Click Select All button* ▢ *to change all rows.*

2 Point to ...... *bottom border of any selected row heading*
Pointer becomes a ↕.

3 Drag .... ↕ *up or down*
Excel displays height on left side of formula bar.

To set row height to fit tallest entry:

• Double-click .... *bottom border of the row's heading*

To set row height to a specific size:

1 Select .... *any cell in row or rows to size*

2 Click .... **Format, Row** ▸, **Height...**

3 Type number (0-409) in .... **Row Height:** [ ]
NOTE: *Number represents height in points.*

4 Click .... [OK]

Hide Columns (by Dragging)

To hide one column:

1 Point to . . . . *right border of column heading*
Pointer becomes a ↔.

2 Drag . . . . ↔ *left*
to column's left border.
Excel displays a bolded column heading border where a column is hidden.

To hide multiple columns:

1 Select . . . . *columns*

2 Point to . . . . . *right border of any selected column heading*
Pointer becomes a ↔.

3 Drag . . . . ↔ *left*
to column's left border.
Excel displays a bolded column heading border where a column is hidden.

Hide Columns (Using Menu)

1 Select . . . . *any cells in column(s) to hide*

2 Click . . . . **F**ormat, **C**olumn ▸, **H**ide
Excel displays a bolded column heading border where a column is hidden.

Show Hidden Columns (by Dragging)

1 Point . . . . *just right of bolded column heading border*
Pointer becomes a ⇥.

2 Drag . . . . ⇥ *right*

Show Hidden Columns (Using Menu)

1 Select . . . . *surrounding columns*

2 Click . . . . **F**ormat, **C**olumn ▸, **U**nhide

Hide Rows (by Dragging)

To hide one row:

1 Point to . . . . ***bottom border of row heading***
Pointer becomes a ↕.

2 Drag . . . . ↕ ***up***
to row's top border.
Excel displays a bolded row heading border where a row is hidden.

To hide multiple rows:

1 Select . . . . ***rows***

2 Point to . . . . . . ***bottom border of any selected row heading***
Pointer becomes a ↕.

3 Drag . . . . ↕ ***up***
to row's top border.
Excel displays a bolded row heading border where a row is hidden.

Hide Rows (Using Menu)

1 Select . . . . ***any cells in row(s) to hide***

2 Click . . . . **F**o**rmat, Row** ▸, **Hide**
Excel displays a bolded row heading border where a row is hidden.

Show Hidden Rows (by Dragging)

1 Point . . . . ***just below bolded row heading border***
Pointer becomes a ⇕.

2 Drag . . . . ⇕ ***down***

Show Hidden Rows (Using Menu)

1 Select . . . . ***surrounding rows***

2 Click . . . . **F**o**rmat, Row** ▸, **Unhide**

Align Data in Cells (Using Toolbar)

1 Select .... *cell(s) containing data to align*

FROM FORMATTING TOOLBAR

2 Click .... *Align Left button* 📄

   OR

   Click .... *Center button* 📄

   OR

   Click .... *Align Right button* 📄

Align Data in Cells (Using Menu)

Aligns data horizontally or vertically in their cells.

1 Select .... *cell(s) containing data to align*

2 Click .... **Format, Cells...**

   OR

   a Right-click .... *any selected cell*

   b Click .... **Format Cells...**

3 Click .... | Alignment |

To align data horizontally:

• Select .... *Horizontal option:*
   General (default alignment),
   Left, Center, Right,
   Fill (cell appears filled with its contents),
   Justify (aligns wrapped text right and left),
   Center across selection.

To align data vertically:

• Select .... *Vertical option:*
   Top, Center, Bottom,
   Justify (aligns and wraps text evenly within its vertical limits)

4 Click .... | OK |

Wrap Text in a Cell

Wraps text to fit in cell. The row height changes to accommodate the text.

1 Select . . . . *cell(s) containing text to wrap*
2 Click . . . . **Format, Cells...**
   OR
   a Right-click . . . . *any selected cell*
   b Click . . . . **Format Cells...**
3 Click . . . . Alignment
4 Select . . . . ☐ **Wrap Text**
5 Click . . . . OK

Justify Text in Cells

Justifies text to fit evenly within border(s) of cell. It wraps text if text has not been wrapped before.

1 Select . . . . *cell(s) containing text to justify*
2 Click . . . . **Format, Cells...**
   OR
   a Right-click . . . . *any selected cell*
   b Click . . . . **Format Cells...**
3 Click . . . . Alignment
4 Select . . . . ◯ **Justify**
   in Horizontal group.
   AND/OR
   Select . . . . ◯ **Justify**
   in Vertical group.
5 Click . . . . OK

Justify Text to Fill a Range

To arrange text in consecutive rows to fill a selected range:

1 Select . . . . *cells containing text to arrange*
NOTE: Cells must be in consecutive rows.

To arrange text over larger area,
• Extend selection to include . . . . *range of empty cells*
where text will distributed.

2 Click . . . . **Edit, Fill ▸, Justify**
Excel redistributes text to evenly fill selection.

To split lengthy text in one cell to fit evenly in selected cells:

1 Select . . . . *cell containing text to split*
and extend selection down to include . . . . *range of empty cells*
below text into which text will be distributed.

2 Click . . . . **Edit, Fill ▸, Justify**
Excel divides text in cell evenly among selected cells.

Center Data Across Columns

Centers data in left-most cells of a selection, across blank cells to the right.
The centered data will remain in original cell(s).

1 Select . . . . *cell(s) in one column containing data to center*
and . . . . *adjacent blank cells to the right*

2 Click . . . . *Center Across Columns button*
Excel centers the data across selection of blank cells.

Change Orientation of Data in Cells

1 Select .... *cell(s) containing data*
2 Click .... F**o**rmat, C**e**lls...
   OR
   a Right-click .... *any selected cell*
   b Click .... **Format Cells...**
3 Click .... | Alignment |
4 Click .... *Orientation option*
5 Click .... | OK |

Change Font (Using Toolbar)

1 Select .... *cells* or *characters in cells*
2 Select desired font in .... | Arial ⬆ |
   on Formatting toolbar, where *Arial* is the name of current font.

Change Font Size (Using Toolbar)

1 Select .... *cells* or *characters in cells*
2 Enter or select a number in .... | 10 ⬆ |
   on Formatting toolbar, where *10* is the point size of current font.

Change Font Color (Using Toolbar)

1 Select .... *cells* or *characters in cells*
2 Click .... *displayed Font Color option* | 🅣 ⬆ |
   to apply it to selection.
   OR
   a Click .... *Font Color drop-down arrow* | 🅣 ⬆ |
      Excel displays a color palette.
      NOTE: To apply several colors, drag color palette off the toolbar to keep the color palette open.
   b Click .... *desired color on palette*

Change Font (Using Menu)

1 Select . . . . *cells* or *characters in cells*

2 Click . . . . **F̲ormat, C̲ells...**

   OR

   a Right-click . . . . *any selected cell*

   b Click . . . . **Format Cells...**

3 Click . . . . `Font`

To change f̲ont:

• Select a font name in . . . . **F̲ont** list

To change font s̲tyle:

• Select a font style in . . . . **F̲ont Style** list
Font Style list items include: Regular, Italic, Bold, Bold Italic

To change font s̲ize:

• Type a point size in . . . . **S̲ize:** `            `

   OR

   Select a point size in . . . . **S̲ize** list

To select an u̲nderline style:

• Select an underline style in . . . . . . **U̲nderline:** `          ±`
None, Single, Double, Single Accounting, Double Accounting

To apply s̲pecial effects:

• Select . . . . *Effects options:*
Strikethrough, Sup̲erscript, Sub̲script

To set font to n̲ormal font style:

• Select . . . . ☐ **N̲ormal Font**

To set font c̲olor:

• Select a color in . . . . **C̲olor** `          ±`

4 Click . . . . `    OK    `

Bold, Italicize, or Underline Text (Using Toolbar)

1 Select .... *cells* or *characters in cells*
FROM FORMATTING TOOLBAR

2 Click .... *Bold button* **B**

OR

Click .... *Italic button* **I**

OR

Click .... *Underline button* **U**

To remove font style:

- Click .... *format button again*

Apply Borders to Cells (Using Toolbar)

1 Select .... *cell(s)*

2 Click .... *displayed Border option*
to apply it to selected cells.

OR

a Click .... *Border drop-down arrow*
Excel displays a border palette.
NOTE: *To apply several border styles, drag border palette off the toolbar to keep the border palette open.*

b Click .... *desired border on palette*

Apply Custom Borders to Cells

1 Select .... *cell(s)*

2 Click .... **Fo̲rmat, Ce̲lls...**

   OR

   a Right-click .... *any selected cell*

   b Click .... **Format Cells...**

3 Click .... ⬜ Border

4 Select a style for border in .... *Sty̲le group*

5 Select border to apply style to in .... *Border group*
   O̲utline, L̲eft, R̲ight, T̲op, B̲ottom

To remove border:

• Click .... *border again*

To change border color:

• Select desired color in .... **C̲olor:** ⬜ ±

6 Repeat steps **4** and **5** for each border.

7 Click .... ⬜ OK

Remove Borders from Cells

• Select .... *cells with borders to remove*

To remove all borders:

• Press .... **Ctrl** + **Shift** + **—**

To remove specific borders:

a Click .... **Fo̲rmat, Ce̲lls...**

b Click .... ⬜ Border

c Click .... *border(s) to remove style from*
   until style is removed.

d Click .... ⬜ OK

Apply Color to Cells (Using Toolbar)

1 Select . . . . *cell(s)*

2 Click . . . . *displayed Color option* 🎨▾
   to apply it to selection.

   OR

   a Click . . . . *Color drop-down arrow* 🎨▾
      Excel displays a color palette.
      NOTE: *To apply several colors, drag color palette off the toolbar to keep the color palette open.*

   b Click . . . . *desired color on palette*

Apply Color or Pattern to Cells (Using Menu)

1 Select . . . . *cell(s)*

2 Click . . . . **Format, Cells...**

   OR

   a Right-click . . . . *any selected cell*

   b Click . . . . **Format Cells...**

3 Click . . . . | Patterns |

To select a color for cells:

   • Click . . . . *desired color on Color palette*

To select a pattern for cells:

   a Select a pattern in . . . . **Pattern** [▾]

   b Select a color for pattern in . . . . **Pattern** [▾]

4 Click . . . . | OK |

Format Number, Date or Time

1 Select . . . . *cell(s)*

2 Click . . . . **Fo̱rmat, Ce̱lls...**

   OR

  a Right-click . . . . *any selected cell*

  b Click . . . . **Format Cells...**

3 Click . . . . | Number |

4 Select a category in . . . . **Ca̱tegory** list
Category list items include: All, Custom, Accounting, Date, Time,
Percentage, Fraction, Scientific, Text, Currency

5 Select a format in . . . . **Fo̱rmat Codes** list

6 Click . . . . | OK |

Apply Common Number Formats (Using Toolbar)

• Select . . . . *cell(s)*

  FROM FORMATTING TOOLBAR

  To apply currency style:

    • Click . . . . *Currency Style button* [$]

  To apply percent style:

    • Click . . . . *Percent Style button* [%]

  To apply the comma style:

    • Click . . . . *Comma Style button* [,]

  To increase or decrease decimal places:

    • Click . . . . *Increase Decimal button* [+.0/.00]

    OR

    Click . . . . *Decrease Decimal button* [.00/+.0]

Create or Delete a Custom Number Format

1 Click .... **F**o**rmat**, **C**e**lls...**

2 Click .... | Number |

To create a new number format:

a Select category for new format in .... **C**ategory list

b Type new number codes or edit
existing number codes in .... **C**o**de:** | |
*NOTE: Editing existing code will not delete the original format.
You can search Excel's Help topic, **format codes, number,** for
valid codes.*

To delete a custom number format:

a Select category containing format in .... **C**ategory list

b Select code to delete in .... **F**ormat **Codes** list

c Click .... | Delete |

3 Click .... | OK |
NOTE: Excel will save the new format when you save the workbook.

Hide Data in Cells

Excel hides the data in the cells. Data can be viewed from formula bar.

1 Select .... *cell(s)*

2 Click .... **F**o**rmat**, **C**e**lls...**
OR

a Right-click .... *any selected cell*

b Click .... **Format Cells...**

3 Click .... | Number |

4 Double-click in .... **C**o**de:** | |
to highlight existing code, and type .... **; ; ;**

5 Click .... | OK |

Clear All Formats Applied to Cells

1 Select . . . . *cell(s)*

2 Click . . . . **Edit, Clear** ▸, **Formats**

Copy Formats (Using Toolbar)

• Select . . . . *cell(s) containing formats to copy*

To copy formats only once:

a Click . . . . **Format Painter button**
on Standard toolbar.
Pointer changes to a ⟨symbol⟩.

b Select . . . . *cell* or *range of cells*
where you want to apply the formats.

To copy formats several times:

a Double-click . . . . **Format Painter button**

on Standard toolbar.
Pointer changes to a ⟨symbol⟩.

b Select . . . . *destination cell(s)*

c Repeat step **b**, as desired.

d Click again . . . . **Format Painter button**
to end copying.

Create a Style by Example

1   Select . . . . *cell containing desired formats*
2   Click . . . . **Format, Style...**
3   Type a name for style in . . . . **Style Name:** [⬧]
    Excel displays the style's formats in Style Includes box.

    ## To exclude format categories from style:

    • Deselect . . . . **Style Includes options:**
      Number, Font, Alignment, Border, Patterns, Protection
4   Click . . . . [OK]

Create a Style by Defining It

1   Click . . . . **Format, Style...**
2   Type a name for style in . . . . **Style Name:** [⬧]
3   Click . . . . [**Modify...**]
4   Click . . . . **tab of format category to include in style**
    *Tab options include: Number, Alignment, Font, Border,
    Patterns, Protection*
5   Select options for selected category.
6   Repeat steps **4** and **5** for each format category to include.
7   Click . . . . [OK]

    ## To exclude format categories from style:

    • Deselect . . . . **Style Includes options:**
      Number, Font, Alignment, Border, Patterns, Protection

    ## To define and apply style:

    • Click . . . . [OK]

    ## To define style without applying it:

    a   Click . . . . [Add]
    b   Click . . . . [Close]

Redefine a Style by Example

1 Select . . . . *cell containing desired formats*
2 Click . . . . **F̲ormat, S̲tyle...**
3 Type name of style to redefine in . . . . . **S̲tyle Name** [⬧]
4 Click . . . . [A̲dd...]

If Redefine prompt appears,

- Click . . . . [Y̲es]

5 Click . . . . [OK]

Excel redefines style and updates cells formatted with style in worksheet.

Redefine a Style by Defining It

1 Click . . . . **F̲ormat, S̲tyle...**
2 Select name of style to redefine in . . . . **S̲tyle Name** [⬧]

To change formats:

a Click . . . . [M̲odify...]
b Click . . . . *tab of format category to change*
Tab options include: Number, Alignment, Font, Border, Patterns, Protection

c Select options for selected category.
d Repeat steps **b** and **c** for each format category to change.
e Click . . . . [OK]

To exclude format categories from style:

- Deselect . . . . *Style Includes options:*
  N̲umber, F̲ont, A̲lignment, B̲order, P̲atterns, Pr̲otection

3 Click . . . . [OK]
Excel redefines style and updates cells formatted with style in worksheet.

Apply a Style

1 Select .... *cell(s) to apply style to*

2 Click .... **Format**, **Style...**

3 Select name of style to apply in ...... **Style Name:** ⬜ ▣

4 Click .... OK

Copy Styles from Another Workbook

1 Open .... *source and destination workbooks*

2 Select .... *destination workbook*

3 Click .... **Format**, **Style...**

4 Click .... Merge...

5 Select name of source workbook in .... **Merge Styles From** list

6 Click .... OK

If Merge styles message appears:

- Click .... Yes
  to replace styles in destination workbook that have the same name.

  OR

  Click .... No
  to retain styles that have the same names in destination workbook.

  OR

  Click .... Cancel
  to cancel procedure.

7 Click .... OK

Delete a Style

1 Click .... **Format, Style...**

2 Select name of style to delete in ..... **Style Name:** ⬚ ▣
   NOTE: *Normal style cannot be deleted.*

3 Click .... [Delete]

4 Click .... [OK]

AutoFormat Worksheet Data

Applies built-in formats to data in a range, a list, or a pivot table.

1 Select .... *any cell in data block to format*
   NOTE: *The data block could be a list or a pivot table.*

2 Click .... **Format, AutoFormat...**

3 Select desired format in .... **Table Format** list

To exclude parts of format:

   a Click .... [Options >>]

   b Deselect .... **Formats to Apply options:**
      Number, Border, Font, Patterns, Alignment, Width/Height

4 Click .... [OK]

Clear an AutoFormat

1 Select .... *any cell in formatted range*

2 Click .... **Format, AutoFormat...**

3 Select **None** in .... **Table Format** list

4 Click .... [OK]

Access Page Setup

Sets page, margins, headers, footers, and sheet options for printing.

1 Select . . . . **sheet(s) to print**

NOTE: *When printing a group of sheets of different types, the settings you select will affect only the active sheet and all sheets of the same type. Therefore, you should repeat these steps for each sheet type when printing a group.*

OR

Select . . . . **cells to print**

To access Page Setup directly:

• Click . . . . **File, Page Setup...**

To access Page Setup from Print Preview:

a Click . . . . **Print Preview button** 🔍
on Standard toolbar.

b Click . . . . `Setup...`

To access Page Setup from Print dialog box:

a Click . . . . **File, Print...**

If printing a range or setting print area or titles,
(See page 159 for information about print areas and titles.)

• Select . . . . ○ **Selection**

b Click . . . . `Page Setup...`

2 Select . . . . **Page Setup options:**

Refer to the following topics:

Set Page Options *(page 156) to set print options for page orientation, scaling of data on page, paper size, print quality, first page number.*

Set Print Margins *(page 157) to set print options for page margins, header and footer margins, and center data on page.*

Set Header and Footer Options *(page 158) to set up repeating text or codes (such as a page number) to print on the top and bottom of each page.*

Set Print Options for Sheet *(page 159) to set print options for print area, print titles, gridlines, notes, row and column headings, black and white printing, page order.*

Set Print Options for Chart *(page 161) to set chart size and print quality.*

Set Page Options

*Sets page orientation, scaling of data on page, paper size, print quality,
first page number.*

1 Access (page 155) .... ***Page Setup***

2 Click .... [Page]

NOTE: Available options will depend on the currently selected printer.

To set page orientation:

- Select .... ○ **Por_t_rait** or ○ **_L_andscape**

To reduce or enlarge data on printed sheet:

a Select .... ○ **_A_djust to:**

b Type or select percentage (10-400)
to reduce or enlarge data in ...... [⬍] **% normal size**

To fit sheet(s) on a specific number of pages:

*NOTE: Excel ignores manual page breaks when this setting is selected.
Not available for chart sheets.*

a Select .... ○ **_F_it to:**

b Type or select number
of pages in ...... [⬍] **page(s) wide by** [⬍] **tall**

To set paper size:

- Select a paper size in .... **Paper Si_z_e** [⬍]

To set print quality:

- Select desired print resolution in .. **Print _Q_uality** [⬍]

To specify first page number:

- Type **Auto** or a number in .. **F_i_rst Page Number:** [ ]

3 Click .... ***Page Setup tab*** or ***command button***

Page Setup tabs: *Margins, Header/Footer, Sheet/Chart*
Command buttons: *OK, Cancel, _P_rint..., Print Previe_w_, _O_ptions...*

Set Print Margins

Sets page margins, header and footer margins, and centers data on page.

1 Access (page 155) .... ***Page Setup***

2 Click .... | Margins |

To set page margins:

• Type or select number
  for margins in .... **T**op, **B**ottom, **L**eft, **R**ight | ⬍ |

To set header and footer margins:

NOTE: *To prevent data from overlapping, these settings should be less than the top and bottom margin settings.*

• Type or select number for margin in ...... **He**ader | ⬍ |

AND/OR

• Type or select number for margin in ...... **F**ooter | ⬍ |

To set how data is aligned on page:

• Select .... ☐ **Hori**z**ontally** and/or ☐ **V**ertically
  NOTE: *For chart sheets, you must first select Custom from the Chart tab, page 161.*

3 Click .... ***Page Setup tab*** or ***command button***
  Page Setup tabs: *Margins, Header/Footer, Sheet/Chart*
  Command buttons: *OK, Cancel, **P**rint..., Print Previe**w**, Options...*

Set Header and Footer Options

Adds repeating text or special codes to the top or bottom of each page.

1 Access (page 155) .... *Page Setup*

2 Click .... | Header/Footer |

To select a built-in header:

- Select a header in .... **Header** | ⬦ |

To select a built-in footer:

- Select a footer in .... **Footer** | ⬦ |

To customize header or footer:

a Select a header in .... **Header** | ⬦ |

   OR

Select a footer in .... **Footer** | ⬦ |

b Click .... | Custom Header... |

   OR

Click .... | Custom Footer... |

c Click in .... **Section to change**
Sections include: Left, Center, Right

d Type or edit .... *text*

To format header or footer text:

1. Select .... *text*

2. Click .... *Font button* | A |

3. Select .... *Font options*

4. Click .... | OK |

Continued ...

Set Header and Footer Options (continued)

To insert a header or footer code:

1. Place .... *insertion pointer*
2. Click .... *a code button:*

🔢	**Page Number**	*inserts page number code*
📑	**Total Pages**	*inserts total pages code*
📅	**Date**	*inserts current date code*
⊗	**Time**	*inserts current time code*
📄	**Filename**	*inserts filename code*
🖵	**Sheet Name**	*inserts active sheet name code*

  e Repeat steps **c** and **d** for each section to change.

  f Click .... OK

3 Click .... *Page Setup tab* or *command button*
Page Setup tabs: Margins, Header/Footer, Sheet/Chart
Command buttons: OK, Cancel, Print..., Print Preview, Options...

Set Print Options for Sheet

Sets print options for area, titles, gridlines, notes, row and column headings, black and white printing, and page order.

1 Access (page 155) .... *Page Setup*
NOTE: To specify a print area or set repeating print titles, you must access Page Setup from Print dialog box, page 155.

2 Click .... Sheet

To define a print area:

* Select (in worksheet) or
  type reference(s) to print in .... **Print Area** [   ]
  NOTE: Separate each range or range name with a comma. To remove a print area, delete the reference.

To set rows as repeating print titles:

* Select rows (in worksheet) or type reference
  to rows in .... **Rows to Repeat at Top** [   ]
  NOTE: Rows must be adjacent. To remove print titles, delete the reference. **Continued ...**

Set Print Options for Sheet (continued)

To set columns as repeating <u>print titles</u>:
- Select columns (in worksheet) or type reference
  to columns in ...... <u>C</u>olumns to Repeat at Left ▢
  *NOTE: Columns must be adjacent. To remove print titles,
  delete the reference.*

To set printing of <u>gridlines</u>:
- Select or deselect .... ☐ **<u>G</u>ridlines**

To print <u>notes</u>:
a Select .... ☐ **<u>N</u>otes**
b Deselect .... ☐ **Row and Col<u>u</u>mn Headings**

To print <u>notes</u> (with references):
a Select .... ☐ **<u>N</u>otes**
b Select .... ☐ **Row and Col<u>u</u>mn Headings**

To set printing to <u>draft quality</u>:
- Select .... ☐ **Draft <u>Q</u>uality**

To set printing to <u>black and white</u>:
- Select .... ☐ **<u>B</u>lack and White**

To print <u>row and column headings</u>:
- Select .... ☐ **Row and Col<u>u</u>mn Headings**

To set <u>page order</u>:
- Select .... ◯ **<u>D</u>own, then Across**
  OR
  Select .... ◯ **Acro<u>s</u>s, then Down**

3 Click .... *Page Setup tab* or *command button*
  Page Setup tabs: *Margins, Header/Footer, Sheet/Chart*
  Command buttons: *OK, Cancel, <u>P</u>rint..., Print Previe<u>w</u>, Options...*

Set Print Options for Chart

Sets printed chart size and print quality.

1 Enable (page 190) . . . . *chart editing*

2 Access (page 155) . . . . *Page Setup*

3 Click . . . . `Chart`

NOTE: *Available options will depend on the currently selected printer.*

To set printed chart size:

• Select . . . . ○ **U̲se Full Page**

OR

Select . . . . ○ **Scale to F̲it Page**

OR

Select . . . . ○ **C̲ustom**

NOTE: *With Custom selected, you can then align chart, page 157.*

To set print quality of chart

• Select . . . . □ **Draft Q̲uality**

To print chart in black and white:

• Select . . . . □ **Print in B̲lack and White**

4 Click . . . . *Page Setup tab* or *command button*

Page Setup tabs: Margins, Header/Footer, Sheet/Chart
Command buttons: OK, Cancel, P̲rint..., Print Previe̲w, Options...

Print Preview

1 If necessary, select sheet(s) or range(s) to preview and set up page for printing (page 155).
NOTE: If previewing a selected range, a print area or print titles, be sure to access page setup options through the Print dialog box (page 155).

2 Click . . . . **Print Preview button** 🔍
on Standard toolbar.

To view next or previous page:
- Click . . . . **Next** or **Previous**

To view a magnified portion of the page:
- Click . . . . **area of page to magnify**

To return to full page view:
- Click . . . . **any area of page**

To change page settings:
a Click . . . . **Setup...**

b Make page setup selections, as desired (page 155).

To change margin settings and column widths:
a Click . . . . **Margins**

b Drag . . . . **margin handle** or **column handle**
to desired position.
NOTE: Status bar displays size as you drag handle.

To print page:
a Click . . . . **Print...**

b Make print selections, as desired (page 165).

To exit Print Preview:
- Click . . . . **Close**

Manual Page Breaks

NOTE: After you insert or remove a manual page break, Excel adjusts the automatic page breaks that follow it. To display automatic page breaks see Show Automatic Page Breaks, below.

To insert a horizontal page break:
1 Select . . . . *row where new page will start*
2 Click . . . . <u>I</u>nsert, Page <u>B</u>reak

To insert a vertical page break:
1 Select . . . . *column where new page will start*
2 Click . . . . <u>I</u>nsert, Page <u>B</u>reak

To insert a horizontal and vertical page break:
1 Select . . . . *cell where new pages will start*
2 Click . . . . <u>I</u>nsert, Page <u>B</u>reak

To remove a horizontal page break:
1 Select . . . . *a cell immediately below page break*
2 Click . . . . <u>I</u>nsert, Remove Page <u>B</u>reak

To remove a vertical page break:
1 Select . . . . . . *a cell immediately to the right of page break*
2 Click . . . . <u>I</u>nsert, Remove Page <u>B</u>reak

To remove all manual page breaks:
1 Click . . . . *Select All button* ⬜
2 Click . . . . <u>I</u>nsert, Remove Page <u>B</u>reak

Show Automatic Page Breaks
1 Click . . . . <u>T</u>ools, <u>O</u>ptions...
2 Click . . . . `View`
3 Select . . . . ⬜ A<u>u</u>tomatic Page Breaks
4 Click . . . . `OK`

164

Select Printer

1 Click .... **File, Print...**

2 Click .... Printer Setup...

3 Select printer in .... **Printer** list

To change printer settings:

a Click .... Setup...

b Select .... *printer settings*
  NOTE: *Printer settings may include paper source, paper size, memory, orientation (landscape/portrait), graphic resolution, cartridges, fonts, and number of copies.*

c Click .... OK

4 Click .... OK

5 Click .... *command button*
  Command buttons: *OK (to print), Page Setup..., Print Preview*

Print Sheets (Using Toolbar)

1 Select ...... *sheet to print* or *any sheet in group to print*
  NOTE: *Excel will only print the print area (page 159) if you defined one.*

2 Click .... *Print button*
  on Standard toolbar.

Print

Prints workbook data using current page settings (page 155).

1 Select . . . . *range(s) in worksheet(s) to print*
NOTE: *Non-adjacent ranges print on separate pages. This procedure overrides print area defined in* **Set Print Options for Sheet** *(page 159).*

OR

Select . . . . . . *sheet to print* or *any sheet in group to print*
NOTE: *Excel will only print the print area (page 159) if you defined one.*

2 Click . . . . **File, Print**
3 Select . . . . **Print What option:**
Selection, Selected Sheet(s), Entire Workbook
NOTE: *When printing selected sheets or the entire workbook, Excel will print only sheets containing data.*

To set number of copies:

• Type or select number in . . . . **Copies:** [　　]⬍

To set page range to print:

a Select . . . . ◯ **Page(s)**
b Type or select first page number to print in . . **From:** [　　]⬍
c Type or select last page number to print in . . . . **To:** [　　]⬍
4 Click . . . . [OK]

Create or Edit a Report

NOTE: To create a report you must first install Report Manager.
See **Install or Remove an Add-In,** *page 173.*

1 Click . . . . **File, Print Report...**

2 a Click . . . . `Add...`
     to create a report.

   b Type a name for report in . . . . **Report Name:** [   ]

   OR

   a Select name of report to edit in . . . . **Reports** list

   b Click . . . . `Edit...`

To create sections for the report:

   a Select sheet for section in . . . . **Sheet:** [↕]

   b If desired, select view for section in . . . . **View:** [↕]

   c If desired, select scenario for section in . . **Scenario:** [↕]

   d Click . . . . `Add`

   e Repeat steps **a-d** for each section to create.

To change print order of a report section:

   a Select section to move in . . . . . **Sections In This Report** list

   b Click . . . . `Move Up`

   OR

     Click . . . . `Move Down`

To delete a report section:

   a Select section to delete in . . . . . **Sections In this Report** list

   b Click . . . . `Delete`

To number report pages consecutively:

   • Select . . . . ☐ **Use Continuous Page Numbers**

3 Click . . . . `OK`

4 Click . . . . `Print...`

   OR

     Click . . . . `Close`

Print Report

1 Click .... **File, Print Report...**

2 Select name of report to print in .... **Reports** list

3 Click .... `Print...`

4 Type number of copies to print in .... **Copies:** ☐

5 Click .... `OK`

Name a View of a Worksheet

NOTE: Excel saves named views with the worksheet. Views can be printed, displayed, or added to a report.

1 If desired, define (page 159) .... ***print area for view***

2 Set .... ***display options for view***
NOTE: Excel stores the following settings: window size, window position, active cell, frozen panes, frozen titles, outlining, zoom percentage, print settings, hidden columns and rows, and many view options.

3 Click .... **View, View Manager...**
*NOTE: If View Manager does not appear on the View menu, see **Install or Remove an Add-In**, page 173.*

4 Click .... `Add...`

5 Type name for view in .... **Name:** ☐

To exclude current print settings from view:

• Deselect .... ☐ **Print Settings**

To exclude hidden columns and rows from view:

• Deselect .... ☐ **Hidden Rows & Columns**

6 Click .... `OK`

Display a View of a Worksheet

1 Select ...... *worksheet containing named view to display*

2 Click .... <u>V</u>iew, <u>V</u>iew Manager...

3 Select name of view to display in .... <u>Vi</u>ews list

4 Click .... [<u>S</u>how]

Delete a View of a Worksheet

1 Select .... *worksheet containing named view to delete*

2 Click .... <u>V</u>iew, <u>V</u>iew Manager...

3 Select name of view to delete in .... <u>Vi</u>ews list

4 Click .... [<u>D</u>elete]

5 Click .... [OK]
to confirm deletion.

6 Click .... [Close]

Print a View of a Worksheet

1 Select .... *worksheet containing named view to print*

2 Click .... <u>V</u>iew, <u>V</u>iew Manager...

3 Select name of view to print in .... <u>Vi</u>ews list

4 Click .... [<u>S</u>how]

5 Click .... *Print button* 🖨
on Standard toolbar.

Split Worksheet into Panes (Using Split Boxes)

Provides simultaneous scrolling of up to four panes. You can freeze panes (page 170) to prevent top, left or both panes from scrolling.

NOTE: *If the scroll bars are not displayed, see* **Set View Options,** *page 173.*

1 Point to . . . *horizontal split box* ▬ or *vertical split box* ▐
on scroll bar.

Pointer becomes a ⥮ *or* ⬌.

2 Drag . . . . ⥮ *or* ⬌ *along scroll bar*
until split bar is in desired position.

Split Worksheet into Panes (Using Menu)

Provides simultaneous scrolling of up to four panes. You can freeze panes (page 170) to prevent top, left or both panes from scrolling.

1 Select . . . . *row*
below which horizontal split will occur.

OR

Select . . . . *column*
to right of which vertical split will occur.

OR

Select . . . . *cell below and to the right*
of which horizontal and vertical split will occur.

2 Click . . . . **Window, Split**

Remove Split Bars

• Double-click . . . . *any part of split bar*

OR

Click . . . . **Window, Remove Split**

Adjust Worksheet Panes

1 Point to ... *horizontal split box* ▬ or *vertical split box* ▌
on scroll bar.
Pointer becomes a ↕ *or* ‖▸.

2 Drag .... ↕ *or* ‖▸ *along scroll bar*
until split bar is in desired position.

Move between Worksheet Panes

• Click .... *desired pane*
OR
Press .... `F6`
until active cell is in desired pane.

Freeze Panes on a Split Worksheet

Locks top and/or left pane when scrolling.

• Click .... <u>W</u>indow, <u>F</u>reeze Panes

Unfreeze Panes

• Click .... <u>W</u>indow, Un<u>f</u>reeze Panes

Freeze Titles

Locks display of title row and/or title column on the screen. This procedure is for a worksheet that has not been split into panes.

1 Select . . . . *row*
below horizontal titles to freeze.

OR

Select . . . . *column*
to right of vertical titles to freeze.

OR

Select . . . . *cell below and to the right*
of horizontal and vertical titles to freeze.

2 Click . . . . **Window, Freeze Panes**

Unfreeze Titles

• Click . . . . **Window, Unfreeze Panes**

Display a Sheet Full Screen

Maximizes the sheet window and removes the status bar as well as any toolbars.

1 Select . . . . **sheet to view full screen**

2 Click . . . . **View, Full Screen**
Excel displays sheet full screen and the Full Screen button on a toolbar.

End Full Screen View

• Click . . . . **Full Screen button** 🔲

OR

Click . . . . **View, ✓ Full Screen**

172

Zoom (Using Toolbar)

Changes the scale of worksheet(s), chart sheet(s) or selected range of cells.

To set magnification for worksheets or chart sheets:

NOTE: *To set a zoom percentage for chart sheets, you must first deselect the Sized with Window option from the View menu (page 173).*

1 Select . . . . *sheet(s) to scale*

2 Enter a number (10-400), or
select a zoom percentage in . . . . `100%  ↧`
on Standard toolbar, where *100%* is the current setting.

To fit a range of cells to the current window size:

1 Select . . . . *range of cells to magnify*

2 Select **Selection** in . . . . `100%  ↧`
on Standard toolbar, where *100%* is the current setting.

Zoom (Using Menu)

Changes the scale of worksheet(s), chart sheet(s) or selected cells.

To set magnification for worksheets or chart sheets:

NOTE: *To set a zoom percentage for chart sheets, you must first deselect the Sized with Window option from the View menu (page 173).*

1 Select . . . . *sheet(s) to scale*

2 Click . . . . **V̲iew, Z̲oom...**

3 Select . . . . *Magnification option:*
200̲%, 1̲00%, 7̲5%, 5̲0%, 2̲5%

  OR

  a Select . . . . ○ **C̲ustom**

  b Type zoom percentage (10-400) in . . . . `        ` %

4 Click . . . . `  OK  `

To fit a selected range to the current window size:

1 Click . . . . **V̲iew, Z̲oom...**

2 Select . . . . ○ **F̲it Selection**

3 Click . . . . `  OK  `

Set View Options

Sets display of many workspace and window elements.

1 Click . . . . **Tools, Options...**

2 Click . . . . | View |

To set general view options:

- Select or deselect . . . . **Show options:**
  Formula Bar, Status Bar, Note Indicator, Info Window
  NOTE: *These selections are not saved with workbook.*

To set view of graphic objects:

- Select or deselect . . . . **Objects options:**
  Show All – select to show all graphic objects.
  Show Placeholders – select to show gray rectangles where pictures
       and embedded charts will appear when printed.
  Hide All – select to hide graphic objects. Hidden objects will not print.

To set view of window options:

- Select or deselect . . . . **Window options:**
  Automatic Page Breaks, Formulas, Gridlines, Gridline Color,
  Row & Column Headers, Outline Symbols, Zero Values,
  Horizontal Scroll Bar, Vertical Scroll Bar, Sheet Tabs

3 Click . . . . | OK |

Install or Remove an Add-In

Add-ins are programs or functions you can add to Excel menus.
They include Analysis ToolPak, AutoSave, Microsoft ODBC Function,
Microsoft Query, Report Manager, Slide Show, Solver and View Manager.

1 Click . . . . **Tools, Add-Ins...**

2 Select or deselect add-ins in . . . . **Add-Ins Available** list
  NOTE: *You can click the Browse button to*
  locate add-ins in other directories.

3 Click . . . . | OK |

Protect a Workbook

Prevents user from changing the way a workbook is arranged or displayed.

1 Select or open . . . . **workbook to protect**

2 Click . . . . . . **Tools, Protection** ►, Protect **W**orkbook...

To set password protection:

• Type password in . . . . **P**assword (optional): [   ]

To protect workbook structure:

Prevents sheets from being inserted, deleted, renamed, moved, hidden or unhidden.

• Select . . . . ☐ **Structure**

To protect workbook windows:

Prevents windows from being closed, sized, moved, hidden or unhidden.

• Select . . . . ☐ **Windows**

3 Click . . . . [OK]

If a password was typed,

a Retype password in . . . . [   ]

b Click . . . . [OK]

Unprotect a Workbook

1 Select or open . . . . **workbook to unprotect**

2 Click . . . . **Tools, Protection** ►, Unprotect **W**orkbook...

If workbook is password protected,

a Type password in . . . . **P**assword: [   ]

b Click . . . . [OK]

Protect a Sheet

Prevents changes to locked cells, graphic objects, embedded charts in a worksheet or chart items in a chart sheet. By default, all cells and objects in a worksheet are locked (page 176).

1 Select . . . . **sheet to protect**

2 Click . . . . **Tools, Protection** ▸, **Protect Sheet...**

To password protect sheet:
• Type password in . . . . **Password (optional):** ⬚

To protect cell contents and chart items:
• Select . . . . ☐ **Contents**

To protect graphic objects:
• Select . . . . ☐ **Objects**

To protect scenarios:
• Select . . . . ☐ **Scenarios**

3 Click . . . . `OK`

If a password was typed,
a Retype password in . . . . ⬚

b Click . . . . `OK`

Unprotect a Sheet

1 Select . . . . **sheet to unprotect**

2 Click . . . . **Tools, Protection** ▸, **Unprotect Sheet...**

If sheet is password protected,
a Type password in . . . . **Password:** ⬚

b Click . . . . `OK`

Lock Cells or Graphic Objects

Unlocks or locks specific cells or graphic objects. By default, all cells and objects in a worksheet are locked. Locking takes effect when a sheet is protected (page 175).

1 If necessary, unprotect (page 175) .... ***sheet***

2 Select .... ***cell(s)*** or ***graphic object(s)*** to unlock or lock.

3 a Click .... **Format**

   b Click ...... **Cells...** or **Object...** or **Selected Object...**
   NOTE: *Press **Ctrl+1** to access Format options quickly.*

4 Click .... [Protection]

5 Deselect or select .... ☐ **Locked**

   To unlock/lock text in a text box:
   • Deselect or select .... ☐ **Lock Text**

6 Click .... [OK]

7 Repeat steps for each cell or object to lock or unlock.

8 Protect (page 175) .... ***sheet***
   to enable locking.

Hide or Unhide Formulas

Hidden formulas will not appear on the formula bar. When you hide a formula, the setting takes effect when a sheet is protected (page 175).

1 If necessary, unprotect (page 175) .... ***sheet***

2 Select .... ***cells containing formulas to hide***

3 Click .... **Format, Cells...**

4 Click .... [Protection]

5 Select or deselect .... ☐ **Hidden**

6 Click .... [OK]

7 Protect (page 175) .... ***worksheet contents***
   to enable hidden formulas.

Graphic Objects

Examples of graphic objects include lines, arcs, arrows, rectangles, ellipses, embedded charts, text boxes, buttons and imported graphics. These objects can be inserted into a worksheet or chart sheet.

Select Graphic Objects

To select one graphic object:

* Click . . . . *object*

  OR

  If a macro has been assigned to the graphic object,

  a Click . . . . **Drawing button**
  on Standard toolbar to show Drawing toolbar.

  b Click . . . . **Drawing Selection button**

  c Click . . . . **any part of object**

  Excel marks object with a selection outline and handles.

  NOTE: *When you have finished editing the object, click the Drawing Selection button again to allow macros to run.*

To select multiple graphic objects:

* Press **Shift** and click . . . . **each object**

  OR

  If a macro has been assigned to any of the graphic objects,

  a Click . . . . **Drawing button**
  on Standard toolbar to show Drawing toolbar.

  b Click . . . . **Drawing Selection button**

  c Drag . . . . **selection outline around objects**

  To add or remove objects:

  * Press **Shift** and click . . . . **each object**

  Excel marks object(s) with a selection outline and handles.

  NOTE: *When you have finished editing the objects, click the Drawing Selection button again to allow macros to run.*

Create a Text Box

1 Click . . . . **Text Box button** 🔲
on Standard toolbar.
Pointer becomes a ╂.

2 Position . . . . ╂
where corner of box will be.

To create a box without constraints:

*   Drag . . . . **box outline**
    until desired size is obtained.

To create a square box:

*   Press **Shift** and drag . . . . **box outline**
    until desired size is obtained.

To create a box and align it to gridlines:

*   Press **Alt** and drag . . . . **box outline**
    until desired size is obtained.

3 Type . . . . **text as desired**

4 Click . . . . **outside text box**
to return to normal operations.

Edit Text in a Text Box

1 Select (page 177) . . . . **text box**

To replace existing text with new text:

*   Type . . . . **new text**

To edit existing text:

NOTE: If text is linked to a worksheet cell, edit from within the formula bar.

a Click . . . . **desired character position**

b Insert and delete . . . . **characters as desired**

2 Click . . . . **outside text box**
to return to normal operations.

Link Text Box Text to Contents of a Cell

1 Select (page 177) . . . . *text box*

2 Click in . . . . *formula bar*

3 Type . . . . ▣
then select (in worksheet) or type . . . . *cell reference*
EXAMPLE: =A4

4 Enter . . . . ⏎

Change Font in Text Box

1 Select (page 177) . . . . *text box*

2 Drag . . . . *highlight over text to format*
NOTE: *If text is linked to a worksheet cell,
you cannot format partial text.*

3 Click . . . . **Fo̲rmat, Obj̲ect...** or **S̲elected Object...**
NOTE: *You can also click buttons on the
Formatting toolbar to format the text quickly.*

4 Select . . . . *Font options*
(See Change Font (Using Menu), page 144.)

5 Click . . . . `  OK  `

Change Text Alignment in Text Box

1 Select (page 177) .... ***text box***
NOTE: Do not click text in text box.

2 Click .... **Fo̲rmat, Obje̲ct...** or **S̲elected Object...**
NOTE: You can also click buttons on the Formatting toolbar to align the text quickly.

3 Click .... | Alignment |

To align text horizontally:

• Select .... ***Horizontal option:***
L̲eft, C̲enter, R̲ight, J̲ustify

To align text vertically:

• Select .... ***Vertical option:***
T̲op, C̲enter, B̲ottom, Justif̲y

To change orientation of text:

• Select .... ***Orientation option***

To set automatic sizing of text box to fit text:

• Select or deselect .... ☐ **A̲utomatic Size**

4 Click .... | OK |

Draw Graphic Objects

Draws objects such as rectangles and ellipses.

1 Click .... ***Drawing button*** 🖉
on Standard toolbar to show Drawing toolbar.
*NOTE: You can rest pointer on a button
in the Drawing toolbar to show its name.*

2 Click .... ***desired drawing tool***
on Drawing toolbar.
Pointer becomes a ╋ and the status bar displays instructions.

3 Point to ...... ***an area where a corner of object will begin***

4 Drag .... ***object's outline***
until desired size and shape is obtained.

Change Border or Fill of Graphic Objects

1 Select (page 177) .... *graphic object(s)*

2 Click .... **Format, Object...** or **Selected Object...**
NOTE: You can double-click object to quickly access format options.

3 Click .... | Patterns |

To change line or border style:

* Select .... *Line or Border options:*
A̲utomatic — to return object to default setting.
N̲one — to make selection invisible.
S̲hadow — to add shadow to rectangles, ellipses, charts or text boxes.
R̲ound Corners — to round corners of rectangles, charts and text boxes.
C̲ustom — to allow for custom formatting.

If Custom,

  a Select line or border style in .... **S̲tyle:** | ⬥ |
  b Select line or border color in .... **C̲olor:** | ⬥ |
  c Select line or border thickness in .... **W̲eight:** | ⬥ |

To change or add an arrow style to a line:

* Select .... *Arrowhead options:*
St̲yle, Wi̲dth, Le̲ngth
NOTE: To add an arrow to a line, you must first select an arrow style before selecting a width or length.

To fill object with color or pattern:

* Select .... *Fill options:*
A̲utomatic — to return object to default setting.
N̲one — to remove fill.
Color palette — to add fills to rectangles, ellipses, charts or text boxes.
P̲attern — to add a pattern to selection. To color the pattern, select
   P̲attern again.

4 Click .... | OK |

Move Graphic Objects

1 Select . . . . *graphic object(s)* or *chart item*

2 Point to . . . . *border of any selected object*
Pointer becomes a ↖ *when positioned correctly.*

3 Drag . . . . *border outline*
to desired position.

   OR

   Press **Alt** and drag . . . . *border outline*
   to align object to gridlines.

Copy Graphic Objects

1 Select . . . . *graphic object(s)*

2 Point to . . . . *border of any selected object*
Pointer becomes a ↖ *when positioned correctly.*

3 Press **Ctrl** and drag . . . . *border outline*
to desired position.

   OR

   Press **Ctrl+Alt** and drag . . . . *border outline*
   to align object to gridlines.

Size Graphic Objects

1 Select . . . . *graphic object(s)* or *chart item*

2 Point to . . . . *selection handle*
on side of border to size.
Pointer becomes a ↘ ↔ ↗ ↕ *when positioned correctly.*
NOTE: *To size object proportionally, point to corner selection handle.*

To size object without constraints:

• Drag . . . . *border outline*
  until desired size is obtained.

To size object and align to gridlines:

• Press **Alt** and drag . . . . *border outline*
  until desired size is obtained.

Delete Graphic Objects

1 Select (page 177) .... *graphic object(s)*

2 Press .... Del

Overlap Graphic Objects

1 Select (page 177) .... *graphic object(s)*

2 Click .... *Drawing button*
on Standard toolbar to show Drawing toolbar.

3 Click .... *Bring To Front button*

OR

Click .... *Send To Back button*

Group or Ungroup Graphic Objects

1 Select (page 177) .... *graphic objects to group*

OR

Select .... *grouped objects to ungroup*

2 Click .... *Drawing button*
on Standard toolbar to show Drawing toolbar.

3 Click .... *Group Objects button*

OR

Click .... *Ungroup Objects button*

Set Properties of Graphic Objects

Sets objects to move and size with underlying cells or chart. Sets print property of object.

1 Select (page 177) .... *graphic object(s)*

2 Click .... **Format, Object...** or **Selected Object...**

3 Click .... | Properties |

4 Select .... *Object Positioning option:*
Objects in worksheets:
Move and Size with Cells (default) — to move and size object with
    underlying cells.
Move but Don't Size with Cells — to move object with underlying cells.
Don't Move or Size with Cells — object is independent of underlying cells.
Objects in charts:
Size with chart, Don't size with chart

To enable or disable printing of object:

• Select or deselect .... ☐ **Print Object**

5 Click .... | OK |

Insert Graphic File (Picture)

Inserts a graphic file into Excel. The supported file formats (such as .BMP and PCX) will depend upon the filters selected when you installed Excel. You can add or remove these filters by running Excel Setup.

1 Select .... *upper-left cell*
where graphic will be inserted.

OR

Enable (page 190) .... *chart editing*

2 Click .... **Insert, Picture...**

3 Select .... *graphic file*
(See Select Drive, Directory, or File(s), page 11.)

To preview picture before inserting it:

• Select .... ☐ **Preview Picture**

4 Click .... | OK |

Copy a Picture of Cells, Graphic Objects or Chart

Pictures are not linked to the source data.

1 Select . . . . *cell(s)* or *object(s)* or *chart*
to copy as a picture.
NOTE: The chart can be on a sheet or an embedded chart.
If graphic objects are within the cells you select, they too will be copied.

2 Press **Shift** and click . . . . **Edit, Copy Picture...**

3 Select . . . . ○ **As Shown on Screen**
to copy selection as it currently appears on screen.

OR

Select . . . . ○ **As Shown when Printed**
to copy selection as it would appear when printed.

To select a graphic format:

- Select . . . . ○ **Picture** or ○ **Bitmap**
NOTE: The Picture format lets you view the image on
systems with display types different from the one it was created on.

4 Click . . . . ▭ OK ▭

5 Select . . . . *upper-left cell* or *object*
in worksheet to receive picture.

OR

Open . . . . *application to receive picture*

6 Click . . . . **Edit, Paste**
NOTE: Scaling values will appear in formula bar to
assist you when you size the object.

Include Graphic Objects in a Sort

If sorting <u>rows</u>,

1 Size (page 182) .... ***graphic objects***
so they are no taller than a single row.

2 Select .... ***cells containing data and objects to sort***

3 Sort (page 119) .... ***selection***

If sorting <u>columns</u>,

1 Size (page 182) .... ***graphic objects***
so they are no wider than a single column.

2 Select .... ***cells containing data and objects to sort***

3 Sort (page 119) .... ***selection***

Draw a Straight Line or Arrow

1 Click .... ***Drawing button*** 🖊
on Standard toolbar to show Drawing toolbar.

2 Click .... ***Line button*** ◿

OR

Click .... ***Arrow button*** ◥

Pointer becomes a $+$.

3 Position .... $+$
where line will begin.

To create line without any constraints:

- Drag .... ***line***
until desired size and direction is obtained.

To create horizontal, vertical or 45 degree lines:

- Press **Shift** and drag .... ***line***
until desired size and direction is obtained.

To create a line and align it to nearest gridlines:

- Press **Alt** and drag .... ***line***
until desired size and direction is obtained.

Create a Chart

1 Select .... *cells containing data to plot*

2 a Click .... <u>I</u>nsert, C<u>h</u>art ▶

  b Click .... <u>O</u>n This Sheet or <u>A</u>s New Sheet
  NOTE: You can also click the 📊 *(ChartWizard button) on the Standard toolbar to create an embedded chart on the worksheet.*

If On This Sheet,
Pointer becomes a ⁺ᵢₗₐ.

  • Drag .... *chart outline to desired size*
  NOTE: To create a square chart, press Shift while dragging chart outline. To align chart with cell structure, press Alt while dragging chart outline.

ChartWizard - Step 1 of 5
3 If necessary, select (in worksheet) or type
reference to cells to plot in .... <u>R</u>ange: ⬚

4 Click .... ⬚ Next >

ChartWizard - Step 2 of 5
5 Click .... *a chart type*

6 Click .... ⬚ Next >

ChartWizard - Step 3 of 5
7 Click .... *a chart format*

ChartWizard - Step 4 of 5
8 Select .... *chart options:*

To change how to plot data series:

  • Select .... ◯ <u>R</u>ows or ◯ <u>C</u>olumns
  Excel shows the result of your selections in a sample chart.

To specify rows or columns to use for axis labels, legend text or chart title:

  • Select number of rows/columns in ...... <u>U</u>se First: ⬚ ⬧
  NOTE: Options will depend on the chart type. To plot values in first row or column (not use them as labels) select 0 (zero).

9 Click .... ⬚ Next >

Continued ...

Create a Chart (continued)

ChartWizard - Step 5 of 5

10 Select .... *other chart options:*

To add or remove legend:

- Select .... ⟡ Y̲es or ⟡ N̲o

To add a chart title:

- Type title in .... C̲hart Title: ☐

To add axis titles:

- Type titles in .... *provided Axis Titles boxes*
  NOTE: Available options will depend on the chart type.

11 Click .... ☐ Finish

Identify Chart Items

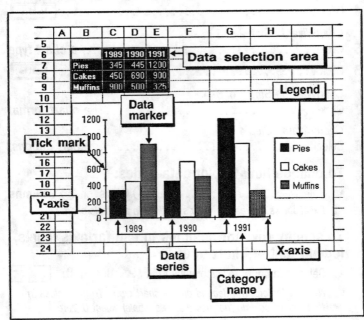

Sample Chart

Illustrated chart items:

- The **data selection area** is a selected range of worksheet cells containing data to plot in a chart.
- A **data marker** (S1P1, S1P2...) is a single symbol or shape in a chart representing one value from the data selection area.
- A **data series** (S1, S2...) is a group of related values in the same row or column in the data selection area. In a chart, the data series is represented by data markers that have the same pattern or color.
- **Category names** are classifications in which data values for each data series are compared.
- The **X-axis** is the horizontal line on which categories of data are usually plotted.
- The **Y-axis** is the vertical line on which data values are usually plotted.
- A **tick mark** is a small line on an axis representing a scaled value or a change in categories.
- A **legend** is a box displaying labels for each data series, and the patterns, symbols or colors of data markers in each data series.

Chart items not illustrated:

- **3-D floor, walls** and **corners** are plot boundaries formed by the X, Y and Z axes of a 3-D chart.
- **Chart lines** are optional lines that include **drop-lines, gridlines, hi-lo lines, series lines, trendlines** and **up/down lines**. These lines can make it easier to read data values or the relationships between values in a chart.
- **Chart text** is text that describes a chart item. Examples of chart text include the **chart title, axes labels, tick labels** on an **axis** and **data marker** and **category name labels**.
- **Error bars** express error amounts relative to each of the data markers in a data series. These bars are used primarily when plotting statistical data.
- **Graphic objects** are items, such as arrows and text boxes, that you can add to any location in the chart to emphasize data.
- The **chart area** is the space inside the chart that includes all items in the chart.
- The **plot area** is the space in which chart axes and data markers are drawn.

Enable Chart Editing

To edit an embedded chart:

- Double-click .... ***embedded chart***
  The chart is surrounded by a thick border with handles, or if the entire chart was not displayed on the sheet, the chart appears in a window.

To edit a chart sheet:

- Select .... ***chart sheet***

A Chart toolbar may appear with these common chart buttons.

	Chart Type
	Default Chart
	ChartWizard
	Horizontal Gridlines
	Legend

Chart Edit Mode Features

Menu bar options

Excel also modifies the menu bar so options specific to the chart type and selected chart item are available. For example:

Insert menu Titles, Data Labels..., Legend, Axes..., Gridlines... Picture..., Trendline..., Error Bars..., New Data...

Format menu Selected Object..., Chart Type..., Auto Format..., 3- D View..., Placement

Shortcut menu options

Excel will display the following shortcut menu items appropriate to the part of the chart you right-click on:

Clear Clear selected item.

Insert: Axes, Data Labels, Error Bars, Gridlines, Titles, Trendline.

Format: Axis, Axis Title, Chart Area, Chart Title, Data Labels, Data Point, Data Series, Error Bars, Gridlines, Legend, Legend Entry, Legend Key, Trendline.

Chart Type, Autoformat, 3-D View, Format Chart Type Group

Name box

Excel displays the selected chart item in the Name box on the left side of the formula bar.

Select Chart Items

You will select chart items prior to selecting commands to change the item in some way.

NOTE: *Excel marks the currently selected chart item with squares, and displays its name in the Name box.*

- Double-click .... *embedded chart*

   OR

   Select .... *chart sheet*

To select next or previous class of chart items:

- Press .... `↑↓`

To select next or previous subitem for selected chart class:

- Press .... `←→`

To select a specific item with the mouse:

- Click .... *chart item*

   To select data series with mouse:

   - Click .... *any data marker in data series*

   To select data marker with mouse:

   a Click .... *any data marker in data series*

   b Click .... *data marker in selected series*

   To select chart area with mouse:

   - Click .... *any blank area outside plot area*

   To select plot area with mouse:

   - Click .... *any blank area inside plot area*

   To select legend or legend subitems with mouse:

   NOTE: *Legend subitems are the legend entry and key.*

   a Click .... *legend*

   b Click .... *subitem in legend*

To deselect a selected chart item:

- Press .... `Esc`

Change Range of Data to Plot

1 Enable (page 190) . . . . *chart editing*

2 Click . . . . *ChartWizard button* 🏦
on Standard toolbar.

3 Select (in worksheet) or type
reference to data to plot in . . . . **R**ange: ▢

4 Click . . . . ▢ Finish ▢

Change Orientation of Data Series to Rows or Columns

1 Enable (page 190) . . . . *chart editing*

2 Click . . . . *ChartWizard button* 🏦
on Standard toolbar.

3 Click . . . . ▢ Next > ▢

4 Select . . . . ◯ **R**ows or ◯ **C**olumns

5 Click . . . . ▢ OK ▢

Change How Rows or Columns in Plot Area Are Used in Chart Text

Depending on the chart type, you can use this procedure to change axis labels, legend entries and the chart title based on text in the plot area.

1 Enable (page 190) . . . . *chart editing*

2 Click . . . . *ChartWizard button* 🏦
on Standard toolbar.

3 Click . . . . ▢ Next > ▢

4 Select number of rows/columns in . . . . **Use First:** ▢ ⬍

   NOTE: Options will depend on the chart type. To plot values in first row or column (not use them as labels) select 0 (zero).

5 Click . . . . ▢ OK ▢

Add Data to Embedded Chart

Adds data in a range of cells to an embedded chart.

1 Select . . . . **range of data to add to chart**
   NOTE: Include category or data series names.

2 Point to . . . . **border of selection**
   Pointer becomes a ↖.

3 Drag . . . . **border outline onto chart**

   If Paste Special dialog box appears,

   a Select options appropriate to your chart and the selection.

   b Click . . . . ▢ OK
      NOTE: If you make the wrong choices in the Paste Special dialog box, select Undo from the Edit menu.

Add Data to Chart Sheet

Adds data in a range of cells to a chart sheet.

1 Select . . . . **range of data to add to chart**
   NOTE: Include category or data series names.

2 Click . . . . **Edit, Copy**

3 Select . . . . **chart sheet**

4 Click . . . . **Edit, Paste**

   If Paste Special dialog box appears,

   a Select options appropriate to your chart and the selection.

   b Click . . . . ▢ OK
      NOTE: If you make the wrong choices in the Paste Special dialog box, select Undo from the Edit menu.

5 Press . . . . Esc
   to end copy.

Add Data to Embedded Chart or Chart Sheet

Adds data in non-adjacent cells to a chart.

1 Enable (page 190) . . . . *chart editing*

2 Click . . . . **Insert, New Data...**

3 Select (in worksheet) or type
reference to cells containing data to add in . . . . **Range:** [   ]

NOTE: Include category or data series names.

If Paste Special dialog box appears,

a Select options appropriate to your chart and the selection.

b Click . . . . [OK]

NOTE: If you make the wrong choices in the Paste Special dialog box, select Undo from the Edit menu.

Change Chart Type (Using Toolbar)

Changes the chart type for an entire chart or a selected data series.
When you change the chart type for a selected series, you are creating
a combination chart.

1 Enable (page 190) . . . . *chart editing*

If changing chart type for a <u>data series</u>,

• Select . . . . *data series*

2 Click . . . . *Chart Type drop-down arrow* [icon]

3 Click . . . . *chart type*

Change Chart Type (Using Menu)

*Changes the chart type for an entire chart, a selected data series or a chart type group (one or more data series formatted as one chart type). When you change the chart type for a selected series, you are creating a **combination** or **overlay chart**.*

1 Enable (page 190) . . . . *chart editing*

To change chart type for a <u>data series</u>:

- Select . . . . *data series*

2 Click . . . . **Fo**rmat, Chart **T**ype...

To change chart type for selected <u>data series</u>:

- Select . . . . ○ **S**elected Series

To change chart type for previously created <u>group</u>:

a Select . . . . ○ **G**roup

b Select group to change in . . . . **G**roup list

To change chart type for <u>entire chart</u>:

- Select . . . . ○ **E**ntire Chart

3 Select . . . . ○ **2-D** or ○ **3-D**

4 Click . . . . *desired chart type*

To select a chart subtype (style):

a Click . . . . `Options...`

b Click . . . . `Subtype`

c Select . . . . *Subtype style*

5 Click . . . . `OK`

Format a Chart Type Group

NOTE: By default, charts contain a single chart type group in which each data series is formatted in the same way. When you change a chart type (pages 194 and 195) for a data series, Excel creates a chart type group for that series. A chart with more than one chart group is often called a combination or overlay chart. When you plot data along a secondary axis (page 196), Excel also creates a chart type group for that series.

1 Enable (page 190) .... ***chart editing***

2 a Click .... **Fo̲rmat**

   b Click .... ***numbered chart type group***
at bottom of menu.

To plot group on primary or secondary axis:
(For charts containing more than one group)

   a Click .... [Axis]

   b Select .... ◯ **P̲rimary Axis** or ◯ **S̲econdary Axis**

To select format options for chart type group:

   a Click .... [Options]

   b Select .... ***Format options for group:***
Overlap, Gap Width, Series Lines, Vary Colors By Point/Slice,
Drop Lines, High-Low, Up-Down Bars, Radar Axis Labels,
Angle of First Slice, Hole Size, Chart Type command, Gap Depth (3-D),
Chart Depth (3-D), Vary Colors by Point (3-D)

To change order of series in chart type group:

   a Click .... [Series Order]

   b Select name of series in .... **S̲eries Order** list

   c Click .... [Move U̲p] or [Move D̲own]

To change subtype (style) for chart type group:

   a Click .... [Subtype]

   b Click .... ***Subtype style***

3 Click .... [OK]

Use Picture as Data Markers

Uses graphics, created in other applications or Excel, as data markers for the following chart types: 2-D Bar, 2-D Column, Line, Radar, and XY Scatter charts.

1 From source application (i.e., Paintbrush or Excel), create, open, or insert (page 184) graphic file.

2 Select . . . . *graphic object* to use as a data marker.

3 Click . . . . **Edit, Copy** to copy image to Clipboard.

4 If source of object is another application, select . . . . *Excel*

5 Enable (page 190) . . . . *chart editing*

6 Select . . . . *data series* or *data marker* to replace with picture.

7 Click . . . . *Paste button* 📋 on Standard toolbar.

NOTE: *To format picture, see **Format Chart Items**, page 210.*

Clear Picture Markers

1 Enable (page 190) . . . . *chart editing*

2 Select . . . . *data series* or *data marker* to clear picture from.

3 Click . . . . **Edit, Clear** ▸, **Formats**

Auto-Format a Chart

Applies a built-in or custom-made format to a chart.

1 Enable (page 190) . . . . *chart editing*
2 Click . . . . **Format, AutoFormat...**
3 Click . . . . ○ **Built-in** or ○ **User-Defined**
4 Select chart type in . . . . **Galleries** list
   Galleries list items include: Area, Bar, Column, Line, Pie, Doughnut,
   Radar, XY (Scatter), Combination, 3-D Area, 3-D Bar, 3-D Column,
   3-D Line, 3-D Pie, 3-D Surface, *or custom names defined by user.*

   If applying a built-in format,
   • Select an autoformat in . . . . **Formats** list
5 Click . . . . `OK`

Create or Delete a Custom Auto-Format

1 Enable (page 190) . . . . *chart editing*
2 Format . . . . *chart as desired*
3 Click . . . . **Format, AutoFormat...**
4 Click . . . . ○ **User-Defined**
5 Click . . . . `Customize...`

   To add a custom format:
   a Click . . . . `Add...`
   b Type name for custom format in . . . **Format Name:**
   c Type description in . . . . **Description:**
   d Click . . . . `OK`

   To delete a custom format:
   a Select format to delete in . . . . **Formats** list
   b Click . . . . `Delete`
   c Click . . . . `OK`
6 Click . . . . `Close`

Guide for Selecting a Chart Type

When plotting:	Chart Types
• relative values over a period of time	**Area**
• emphasize amount of change in values	**Area**
• categories on Y axis	**Bar**
• compare values of items	**Bar**
• values of items and relation to whole	**Stacked Bar**
• changing values for same item at specific times	**Column**
• categories on Y axis	**Column**
• compare items on X axis	**Column**
• values at specific times and relation to whole	**Stacked Column**
• trends	**Line**
• values at regular intervals	**Line**
• emphasize rate of change	**Line**
• emphasize time flow	**Line**
• stock prices	**Line** (Subtype--High-Low-Close)
	Line (Subtype--Open-High-Low-Close)

(Order of data series must correspond to name of chart)

• relation of values to a whole	**Pie**
• one data series	**Pie**
• relation of more than one data series to a whole	**Doughnut**
• values at unrelated intervals	**XY Scatter**
• relationships between numerous values	**XY Scatter**
• scientific data	**XY Scatter**
• best combination for two sets of data	**3-D Surface**
• relationships between large amounts of data	**3-D Surface**

NOTE: *Use 3-D versions of chart types for emphasis and visual appeal:*
3-D Area, 3-D Bar Chart, 3-D Column, 3-D Perspective Column,
3-D Line, 3-D Pie, 3-D Surface

Return Chart to Default Chart Type and Format

The default chart type is the column type with a legend.

1 Enable (page 190) .... *chart editing*

2 Click .... *Default Chart button* 📊
on Chart toolbar.

Set Default Chart Options

NOTE: *Available options will depend upon the chart type and where the chart is located (i.e., embedded or on a chart sheet).*

1 Enable (page 190) .... *chart editing*

2 Click .... **T**ools, **O**ptions...

3 Click .... [Chart]

To set how empty cells are plotted in Line charts:

• Select .... *Empty Cells Plotted as option:*
   Not Plotted (leave gaps) — *to leave gaps in lines when cells are empty.*
   Zero — *to treat blank cells as zero.*
   Interpolated — *to fill in for empty cells with connected lines.*

To set plotting of visible cells:

• Select or deselect .... ☐ **P**lot Visible Cells Only

To set chart sizing with window frame:

• Select or deselect .. ☐ **C**hart Sizes with Window Frame

To change the default chart:

• Select chart type in ... **D**efault Chart Format [⬦]
   NOTE: *Select Built-in to reset chart to original default type.*

To make current chart type the default chart:

a Click .... [**U**se the Current Chart...]

b Type format name in .... **F**ormat Name: [   ]

c Click .... [OK]

4 Click .... [OK]

Display or Hide Axes

1 Enable (page 190) . . . . *chart editing*

2 Click . . . . **Insert, A̲xes...**

3 Select or deselect . . . . ☐ **C̲ategory (X) Axis**

OR

Select or deselect . . . . ☐ **V̲alue (Y) Axis**

If chart is a 3-D chart,

- Select or deselect . . . . *Axis options:*
  C̲ategory (X) Axis, S̲eries (Y) Axis, V̲alue (Z) Axis

4 Click . . . . [OK]

Change Scale on an Axis

For category axes,
- *sets where (X) axis will cross (Y) axis;*
- *sets number of categories between tick mark labels;*
- *sets number of categories between each pair of tick marks;*
- *other options — Value (Y) Axis Crosses Between Categories, Categories in Reverse Order, Value (Y) Axis Crosses at Maximum Category.*

For series axes (value axis),
- *sets minimum and maximum data values displayed on axes;*
- *sets increments between tick marks and gridlines;*
- *sets where (X) axis will cross (Y) axis;*
- *other options — Logarithmic Scale, Values in Reverse Order, Category (X) Axis Crosses at Maximum Value.*

1 Enable (page 190) . . . . *chart editing*

2 Double-click . . . . *axis*

3 Click . . . . [Scale]

4 Select options appropriate to selected axis and chart type.

5 Click . . . . [OK]

Insert Data Labels

Adds data labels to a data series or a specific data marker in a chart.

1 Enable (page 190) . . . . **chart editing**

2 Select (page 191) . . . . **data series** or **data marker**
to which label(s) will be added.

OR

Select . . . . **chart or plot area**
to add labels to all data markers.

3 Click . . . . **Insert, Data Labels...**

4 Select . . . . **Data Labels option:**
None – to remove existing data label.
Show Value – to show value of data point.
Show Percent – to show percentage of part to whole for pie and
doughnut charts.
Show Label – to show category or series name.
Show Label and Percent – to show category or series name and
percentage of part to whole for pie and doughnut charts.

To display legend keys next to data labels:

• Select . . . . ☐ **Show Legend Key next to Label**

5 Click . . . . ⬜ OK ⬜
*NOTE: Data labels are linked to worksheet data and
they can be edited in the worksheet (page 203), edited in
the chart (page 203), formatted (pages 208 and 210) and
moved (page 212).*

Insert Chart Title and Axes Labels

1 Enable (page 190) . . . . **chart editing**

2 Click . . . . **Insert, Titles...**

3 Select . . . . **Attach Text to options:**
*Chart Title, Value (Y) Axis, Category (X) Axis, Second Value (Y) Axis,
Second Category (X) Axis*
NOTE: Available options will depend on chart type.

4 Click . . . . ⬜ OK ⬜
*NOTE: Chart titles and axes labels are not linked to worksheet data,
and they can be edited in the chart (page 203),
formatted (pages 208 and 210) and moved (page 212).*

Edit Chart Text in Chart

With this procedure, you can edit unlinked chart text (such as axis and chart titles, text boxes, and trendline labels) and some linked text (data labels and tick mark labels).

NOTE: *When you edit linked text, Excel removes the link to the worksheet data.*

1 Enable (page 190) . . . . **chart editing**

2 Select . . . . **chart item containing text**

To replace existing text with new text:

a Type . . . . **new text**
   Text appears in formula bar.

b Enter . . . . ⏎

To edit existing text:

a Click . . . . **desired character position in chart item**

b Insert and delete . . . . **characters as desired**

c Click . . . . **anywhere outside of chart item**

Edit Linked Chart Text in Worksheet

When you edit linked text (legend entries, data labels (values or text), and tick mark labels) in the worksheet, Excel automatically updates the chart.

1 Select . . . . **worksheet containing chart data**

2 Edit . . . . **cell containing data label or value**

Change Data Label Options

1 Enable (page 190) .... *chart editing*
2 Double-click .... *data series* or *data marker*
3 Click .... | Data Labels |

To relink edited data labels to worksheet cells:

- Select .... ☐ **Automatic Text**
  NOTE: This option will be available only if
  you edited the text in a data label.

To show or not show legend key with data labels:

- Select or deselect .. ☐ **Show Legend Key next to Label**
4 Click .... | OK |

Link Chart Text to Worksheet Data

Chart text, such as legend entries, data labels and tick mark labels are
automatically linked to the data worksheet cells. You can use this
procedure to link other chart text (such as axis labels, chart titles, text box
text) to the contents of cells in a worksheet.

1 Enable (page 190) .... *chart editing*
2 Select .... *chart item containing unlinked text*
3 Press .... ▤
  Equal sign appears in formula bar.
4 Select (in worksheet) or type .... *reference to cell*
  containing text.
5 Enter .... ⏎

Insert a Legend

1 Enable (page 190) . . . . *chart editing*

2 Click . . . . **Insert, Legend**

OR

Click . . . . *Legend button* 📇

NOTE: *Legend entries are linked to worksheet data and they can be edited in the worksheet (page 203) or in the chart (see below). Legend, legend entries and keys can be formatted (pages 208 and 210). You can also move (page 212) and size (page 212) the legend.*

Edit Legend Entry in Chart

NOTE: *You can also edit legend entries in the worksheet (page 203).*

1 Enable (page 190) . . . . *chart editing*

2 Double-click . . . . *data series for legend to change*

3 Click . . . . | Names and Values |

4 Select reference (in worksheet) containing
series name or type series name in . . . . **Name:** [ ]
NOTE: *If you type a name, the automatic link to the worksheet is ended.*

5 Click . . . . | OK |

Insert or Remove Gridlines

1 Enable (page 190) . . . . *chart editing*

2 Click . . . . **Insert, Gridlines...**

OR

Click . . . . *Horizontal Gridlines button* 📊

If you selected Gridlines from the menu,

a Select or deselect . . . . . *Category (X/Y/Z) Axis options:*
Major Gridlines, Minor Gridlines
NOTE: *Available options depend on chart type.*

b Click . . . . | OK |

Insert or Modify Error Bars

Error bars express error amounts relative to each of the data markers in a data series. These bars are used primarily when plotting statistical data.

1 Enable (page 190) . . . . **chart editing**

2 Select . . . . **data series to receive error bars**

3 Click . . . . **Insert, Error Bars...**

4 Select . . . . **Display option:**
   Both, Plus, Minus, None

5 Select . . . . **Error Amount option:**
   Fixed Value, Percentage, Standard Deviation(s), Standard Error, Custom

   If xy chart,

   a Select . . . . [Y Error Bars]

   b Select . . . . **Display option:**
      Both, Plus, Minus, None

   c Select . . . . **Error Amount option:**
      Fixed Value, Percentage, Standard Deviation(s), Standard Error, Custom

6 Click . . . . [OK]

Change 3-D Walls and Gridlines to 2-D

NOTE: *Chart type must be a 3-D Bar or Column.*

1 Enable (page 190) . . . . **chart editing**

2 Click . . . . **Insert, Gridlines...**

3 Select . . . . ☐ **2-D Walls and Gridlines**

4 Click . . . . [OK]

Insert Trendlines

1 Enable (page 190) . . . . *chart editing*

2 Select . . . . *data series to plot trend for*

3 Click . . . . **Insert, Trendline...**

4 Click . . . . | Type |

5 Select trend type in . . . . **Trend/Registration Type** list
Trend/Registration Type list items include: Linear, Logarithmic,
Polynomial Order, Power, Exponential, Moving Average Period

If Polynomial Order,

- Type or select highest power
  for independent variable in . . . . **Order:** [   ] ⬍

If Moving Average Period,

- Type or select number of periods
  for calculation in . . . . **Period:** [   ] ⬍

6 Click . . . . | OK |

Delete Chart Item

1 Enable (page 190) . . . . *chart editing*

2 Select . . . . *chart item to delete*

3 Press . . . . [Del]
NOTE: If you delete the wrong items, select Undo from the Edit menu.

Other Items You Can Insert in a Chart

*You can add graphic objects, pictures and unattached text boxes to
any chart.*

Format Chart Text

Changes font and alignment of selected text or all text in chart item.

1 Enable (page 190) . . . . **chart editing**

2 Double-click . . . . **chart text** or **legend**
to format entire text.

   OR

   a Select . . . . **chart item**
   to format individual characters.
   NOTE: *You cannot format individual characters if the text
   (i.e., legend text) is linked to worksheet data.*

   b Select . . . . **characters in text to format**

   c Click . . . . **F̲ormat, Selected ...**

To change font:

   a Click . . . . `Font`

   b Select (page 144) . . . . **Font options**

To change alignment and orientation of text:

   a Click . . . . `Alignment`

   b Select . . . . **Orientation option**

3 Click . . . . `OK`

NOTE: *You can also format selected text or text in a selected chart
item by clicking the desired format buttons on the Formatting toolbar.*

Rotate and Elevate a 3-D Chart (by Dragging)

1 Enable (page 190) . . . . **chart editing**

2 Select . . . . **any 3-D corner**

3 Point to . . . . **any corner**
Pointer becomes a ╋.

4 Drag . . . . **chart outline**
until desired view is obtained.
NOTE: *To view data markers as you drag, hold down* **Ctrl** *while
dragging corner.*

Set View Options for a 3-D Chart (Using Menu)

1 Enable (page 190) . . . . *chart editing*

2 Click . . . . **Format, 3-D View...**

To increase or decrease elevation:

- Click . . . . *Elevation buttons* ⬆ or ⬇

To rotate chart left or right:

- Click . . . . *Rotation buttons* ↺ or ↻

To increase or decrease perspective:
(Not available if Right Angle Axes is selected.)

- Click . . *Perspective buttons* ⬎ or ⬏

To lock axes at right angles:

- Select . . . . ☐ **Right Angle Axes**

To scale chart to fill window:
(Available if Right Angle Axes is selected.)

- Select . . . . ☐ **Auto Scaling**

To set height in relation to base of chart:

- Type number (5-500) in . . . . **Height:** ☐ **% of Base**

To preview chart in sheet with current settings:

a Move . . . . *dialog box so that chart is visible*

b Click . . . . **Apply**

To return chart to default settings:

- Click . . . . **Default**

3 Click . . . . **OK**

Format Chart Numbers

1 Enable (page 190) . . . . *chart editing*

2 Double-click . . . . *chart item containing values*

3 Click . . . . | Number |

4 Select a category in . . . . **Category** list
Category list items include: All, Custom, Accounting, Date, Time, Percentage, Fraction, Scientific, Text, Currency

5 Select a format in . . . . **Format Codes** list

To link edited data labels that are values to worksheet data:

● Select . . . . ☐ **Linked to Source**

6 Click . . . . | OK |

Format Chart Items

Formats the following chart items: axis, 3-D floor, 3-D walls, borders, lines, chart area, data series, data markers, error bars, gridlines, legend, legend key, picture markers, plot area, tick marks and trendlines.

1 Enable (page 190) . . . . *chart editing*

2 Double-click . . . . *chart item to format*

3 Click . . . . | Patterns |

NOTE: Available options will depend on the chart item you double clicked.

To format border:

● Select . . . . *Border options:*
Automatic, None, Custom (Style, Color, Weight), Shadow

To format area:

● Select . . . . *Area options:*
Automatic, None, Color, Pattern, Invert if Negative

To format axis:

● Select . . . . *Axis option:*
Automatic, None, Custom (Style, Color, Weight)

Continued ...

Format Chart Items (continued)

To format tick marks:

- Select . . . . *Tick-Mark Labels option:*
  N*o*ne, *L*ow, Hi*g*h, Ne*x*t to Axis

  AND/OR

  Select . . . . *Tick Mark Type options:*
  *M*ajor (None, Inside, Outside, Cross),
  Mino*r* (None, Inside, Outside, Cross)

To format line:

- Select . . . . *Line options:*
  *A*utomatic, *N*one, *C*ustom (*S*tyle, *C*olor, *W*eight), *S*moothed Line

To format markers:

- Select . . . . *Marker options:*
  A*u*tomatic, N*o*ne, *C*ustom (St*y*le, *F*oreground, *B*ackground)

To format picture markers:

- Select . . . . *Picture Format option:*
  *S*tretch, Sta*c*k, Stack and S*c*ale to (*U*nits/Picture)

4 Click . . . . | OK |

Delete an Embedded Chart

1 Click . . . . *embedded chart*
Handles appear on chart border.

2 Press . . . . |Del|

Delete a Chart Sheet

(See Delete Sheets, page 39.)

Size or Move an Embedded Chart

*(See **Size Graphic Objects**, page 182.*
*See **Move Graphic Objects**, page 182.)*

Protect Embedded Chart

*(See **Protect a Sheet**, page 175.*
*See **Lock Cells or Graphic Objects**, page 176.)*

Protect a Chart Sheet

*(See **Protect a Workbook**, page 174.*
*See **Protect a Sheet**, page 175.)*

Size a Chart's Plot Area or Legend

1 Enable (page 190) . . . . *chart editing*

2 Select . . . . *plot area* or *legend*
   Handles appear on item's border.

3 Point to . . . . *handle on side of item to size*
   Pointer becomes a ↖ ↔ ↗ ↕.

4 Drag . . . . *item outline in direction to size*

Move a Chart Item

You can move the plot area, legend, chart title, data labels and axes labels.

1 Enable (page 190) . . . . *chart editing*

2 Select . . . . *chart item to move*

3 Drag . . . . *chart item outline*

Size a Data Marker to Change a Plotted Value

Changes the value in the chart and the worksheet for the following 2-D chart types: Bar, Column, Line, Pie, and Stacked, as well as doughnut and XY Scatter type charts.

1 Enable (page 190) . . . . *chart editing*

2 Select . . . . *data marker*
representing value to change.

3 Point to . . . . *largest handle of data marker*
Pointer becomes a ↕ *or* ＋.

4 Drag . . . . *marker outline up or down*
Excel displays the value in the Name box.

If marker represents a value that is based on a formula,
The Goal Seek dialog box appears.

   a Select (in worksheet) reference
      to cell that will change in . . **By <u>c</u>hanging cell:** | |

   b Click . . . . [OK]

   c Click . . . . [OK]

Create New Object and Embed It into a Worksheet

Inserts an object you create into another application so you can easily edit it from the source application.

1 Select . . . . *cell where object will be inserted*

2 Click . . . . **Insert, Object...**

3 Click . . . . [Create New]

4 Select source application in . . . . **Object Type** list

To display inserted object as an icon:

• Select . . . . □ **Display as Icon**

To change icon to be displayed:

   a Click . . . . [Change Icon...]

   b Select icon in . . . . **Icon** list

      NOTE: You can click the Browse button to select another source file (i.e., MORICONS.DLL) for the icon.

   c If desired, edit caption in . . . . **Caption:** [   ]

   d Click . . . . [OK]

5 Click . . . . [OK]

6 Create object in . . . . *Application*

7 Double-click . . . . *application's control box* ▭
to close the application.

8 Click . . . . [Yes]

Embed Portion of Existing Object into a Worksheet

1 Open . . . . *application containing object to embed*
 NOTE: *Application must support object linking and embedding
 (i.e., Paintbrush, or Sound Recorder).*

2 Open . . . . *file containing object*

3 Select . . . . *part of document to embed*

4 Click . . . . **Edit, Copy**

5 Run or select . . . . *Excel 5*

6 Select . . . . *cell where object will be inserted*

7 Click . . . . **Edit, Paste Special...**

8 Select . . . . ○ **Paste**

To display object as an icon:

- Select . . . . ☐ **Display as Icon**

   To change icon to be displayed:

   a Click . . . . [Change Icon...]

   b Select icon in . . . . **Icon** list
    NOTE: *You can click the Browse button to select
    another source file (i.e., MORICONS.DLL) for the icon.*

   c If desired, edit caption in . . . . **Caption:** [   ]

   d Click . . . . [OK]

9 Click . . . . [OK]

Embed or Link Portion of Excel Object into Another Application

1 Select . . . . ***part of document to embed or link***
NOTE: *You can select cells, graphic objects or chart.*

If linking object,

- Save and name . . . . ***Excel workbook***

2 Click . . . . **Edit, Copy**

3 Run or select . . . . ***application to receive object***
NOTE: *Application must support object linking and embedding.*

4 Place . . . . ***insertion point in document***

5 Follow application's procedure for embedding or linking an object.

Edit Object Embedded in Worksheet

NOTE: *If object was created on another, connected computer, you can edit it only if the same application exists locally.*

1 Select . . . . ***object to edit***

2 Click . . . . **Edit, Object** ▸, **Edit**

3 Edit . . . . ***object in source application***

4 Double-click . . . . ***application's control box*** |—|
to close the application.

5 Click . . . . | Yes |

Embed Exiting File into a Worksheet

Inserts a file previously created in another application as an object—so you can easily edit the object from the source application.

1 Select .... *cell where object will be inserted*

2 Click .... **I**nsert, **O**bject...

3 Click .... Create from File

4 Select file to embed in .... **File Name** list

NOTE: *To successfully embed the object, the application that created the file must support object linking and embedding (i.e., Paintbrush or Sound Recorder).*

To display inserted object as an icon:

- Select .... ☐ **Display as Icon**

  #### To change icon to be displayed:

  a Click .... Change Icon...

  b Select icon in .... **Icon** list

  NOTE: *You can click the Browse button to select another source file (i.e., MORICONS.DLL) for the icon.*

  c If desired, type caption in .... **Caption:** [ ]

  d Click .... OK

5 Click .... OK

Delete Embedded or Linked Object in Worksheet

1 Select .... *object to delete*

2 Press .... Del

218

218 *Object Linking and Embedding*

Link an Object to a Worksheet

1 Run or select .... *application from which object originates*
NOTE: *Application must support object linking and embedding (i.e., Paintbrush or Sound Recorder).*

2 Create or open .... *file to link*

3 Save and name .... *the file*

4 Select .... *part of file to link*

5 Click .... **Edit, Copy**

6 Run or select .... *Excel 5*

7 Select .... *cell where object will be inserted*

8 Click .... **Edit, Paste Special...**

9 Select .... ○ **Paste Link**

10 Select format to use in .... **As** list

To display linked object as an icon:

- Select .... ☐ **Display as Icon**

  ### To change displayed icon:

  a Click .... Change Icon...

  b Select icon in .... **Icon** list
  NOTE: *You can click the Browse button to select another source file (i.e., MORICONS.DLL) for the icon.*

  c If desired, type caption in .... **Caption:** ☐

  d Click .... OK

11 Click .... OK

Edit Linked Object in Worksheet

1 Select .... *object to edit*

2 Click .... **Edit, Object**

3 Edit .... *object in source application*

4 Save .... *the file*

5 Double-click .... *application's control box* ▭
to close the application.

Manage Linked Objects

1 Open or select ...... *workbook containing linked object(s)*

2 Click .... **Edit, Links...**
Excel lists all source files.

To open source file and edit object:

a Select source file in .... **Source File** list

b Click .... | Open |

To replace source file with another:

a Select source file to replace in .... **Source File** list

b Click .... | Change Source... |

c Select new source file in .... **File Name** list

d Click .... | OK |

To change how linked objects are updated:

a Select source file in .... **Source File** list

b Select .... ○ **Automatic** or ○ **Manual**

To update objects set to manual:

a Select source file in .... **Source File** list

b Click .... | Update Now |

To exit dialog box and return to workbook:

• Click .... | Close |

3 Click .... | OK |

Mail a Workbook

Sends a copy of the open workbook to one or more recipients.

NOTE: *Requires Microsoft Mail, Lotus cc:Mail or other mail programs compliant with Messaging Application Programming Interface (MAPI) or Vendor Independent Messaging (VIM). The recipient must also have Microsoft Excel 5 installed.*

1 Click . . . . **File, Send...**

2 If necessary, sign in to your . . . . **mail system**

If routing slip is attached to workbook,

   a Select . . . . . . ⃝ **Send copy of document without using the Routing Slip**

   b Click . . . . `OK`

3 Send . . . . *message* through your mail system to one or more recipients.

Route a Workbook

Sends a copy of the open workbook all at once or sequentially to more than one recipient, and then routes the workbook back to you.

NOTE: *Requires Microsoft Mail, Lotus cc:Mail or other mail programs compliant with Messaging Application Programming Interface (MAPI) or Vendor Independent Messaging (VIM). The recipient must also have Microsoft Excel 5 installed.*

1 Create or edit (page 221) . . . . **routing slip for workbook**

2 Click . . . . **File, Send...**

3 If necessary, sign in to your . . . . **mail system**

4 Select . . . . ⃝ **Route document to...**

5 Click . . . . `OK`

Create or Edit a Routing Slip

Creates a routing slip that is stored with the workbook. Your mail system will use the instructions in the routing slip when you route the workbook (page 220). You can also route the workbook from the Routing Slip dialog box.

1 Click .... **File, Add/Edit Routing Slip...**

2 If necessary, sign on to your .... *mail system*

To clear routing slip:

• Select .... `Clear`

To add recipients:

a Click .... `Address...`

b Use your mail system to select recipients.
Excel adds recipients to the To list.

To remove a name from To list:

a Select name of recipient to remove in .... **To** list

b Click .... `Remove`

To re-order recipients when sending mail sequentially:

a Select name of recipient to move in .... **To** list

b Click .... `⬆` or `⬇`

c Repeat steps **a** and **b** until list is in desired order.

To change subject text:

• Type subject text in .... **Subject:** `⬚`

To add or edit message text:

• Type message in .... **Message Text:** `⬚`

To route workbook back to you:

• Select .... ☐ **Return When Done**

To receive notification when routing:

• Select .... ☐ **Track Status**

Continued ...

Create or Edit a Routing Slip (continued)

3 Select .... ◯ <u>O</u>ne After Another

OR

Select .... ◯ A<u>l</u>l at Once

4 Click .... [<u>A</u>dd Slip]
   to add slip to the workbook without sending.

OR

   Click .... [<u>R</u>oute]
   to send workbook.

To reset routing slip:

NOTE: After the routed workbook is returned or the last recipient receives it, Excel changes the Clear command button to the Reset button.

• Click .... [R<u>e</u>set]

Receive Routed Workbook

NOTE: *Requires Microsoft Mail, Lotus cc:Mail or other mail programs compliant with Messaging Application Programming Interface (MAPI) or Vendor Independent Messaging (VIM). The recipient must also have Microsoft Excel 5 installed.*

FROM YOUR MAIL PROGRAM

1 Open . . . . *message containing routed workbook file*
NOTE: *The message will indicate that the document has a routing slip and whether or not you should send the message to someone else.*

2 Open . . . . *attached workbook file*
FROM EXCEL 5

3 Read or change . . . . *workbook data*

To send workbook to next recipient:

a Click . . . . **F̲ile, Sen̲d...**
b Select . . . . ○ **Route document to...**
c Click . . . . `OK`

To edit subject, message text or add recipients before sending workbook to next recipient:

a Click . . . . **F̲ile, Edit R̲outing Slip...**
b Make desired changes.
c Click . . . . `Route`

Record a Macro

1   If necessary, mark (page 225) .. ***position for recording macro***

2   **a**   Click .... **Tools, Record Macro** ▶

      b   Click .... **Record New Macro...**

3   Type macro name in .... **Macro Name:** ▢

4   Type description in .... **Description:** ▢

5   Click .... ▢ **Options >>**

To assign macro to Tools menu:

      a   Select .... ▢ **Menu Item on Tools Menu**

      b   Type menu text in .. **Menu Item on Tools Menu:** ▢

To assign a shortcut key for playing back macro:

      a   Select .... ▢ **Shortcut Key**

      b   Type letter in .... **Ctrl +** ▢

To specify where macro will be stored:

*   Select .... ***Store in option:***
  Personal Macro Workbook – macro will always be available.
  This Workbook – macro will only be available in current workbook.
  New Workbook – stores macro in separate workbook.

To set macro language:

*   Select ..... ◯ **Visual Basic** or ◯ **MS Excel 4.0 Macro**

6   Click .... ▢ **OK**
Excel displays a tool bar with a Stop Macro button.

To set references to relative or absolute:

      a   Click .... **Tools, Record Macro** ▶

      b   Select or deselect .... **Use Relative References**

7   Execute .... ***commands to record***

8   Click .... ***Stop Macro button*** ▣
when done.
*Excel adds a module or macro sheet to the end of the existing sheets in
the workbook if you specified This Workbook, above.*

Play Back a Macro

- Press .... *assigned shortcut key*

OR

a Click .... **Tools, Macro...**

b Select macro to run in .... **Macro Name/Reference** list

c Click .... Run

OR

a Click .... **Tools**

b Select .... *assigned macro name*
near bottom of menu.

Mark Position for Recording Macro

Marks starting point in a module where a new macro will be recorded or marks insertion point where recorded actions will be inserted into an existing macro.

1 Select .... *module sheet containing macro*

2 Place .... *insertion point in module*
where macro code will be inserted or new macro will begin.

3 a Click .... **Tools, Record Macro** ▸

b Click .... **Mark Position for Recording**

4 Select .... *sheet and cell where recording will begin*

5 Record macro (page 224) or record actions into existing macro (see below).

Record Actions into Existing Macro

1 Mark (see above) .... *position in existing macro*
where macro code will be inserted.
NOTE: If using MS Excel 4.0 macro language, insert cells in module to receive macro code. (You will need to edit the macro when done.)

2 Click ..... **Tools, Record Macro** ▸, **Record at Mark**

3 Follow steps **6-8** for **Record a Macro**, page 224.

Assign Macro to a Graphic Button

1 Click . . . . *Drawing button* 🔲
  on Standard toolbar to show Drawing toolbar.

2 Click . . . . *Create Button* 🔲
  on Drawing toolbar.
  Pointer becomes a ╂.

3 Drag . . . . *outline of button*
  to desired position in worksheet.

4 Select desired macro in . . . . **Macro/Name/Reference** list

5 Click . . . . | OK |

6 Click in . . . . *button text*

7 Edit . . . . *text in button*

8 Click . . . . *anywhere in worksheet*
  *NOTE: To select a button to which a macro has been assigned, you
  must first click the Drawing Selection button* 🔲 *on the Drawing
  toolbar. This will let you select the button without executing the macro.*

Manage Existing Macros

1 Click . . . . **Tools, Macro...**

2 Select macro name in . . . . **Macro Name/Reference** list

  To edit macro code:

  • Click . . . . | Edit |

  To delete selected Visual Basic macro:

  • Click . . . . | Delete |

  To set options for selected macro:

  a Click . . . . | Options... |

  b Select . . . . *Macro options:*
    *Description, Assign to Menu Item on Tools Menu,
    Assign to Shortcut Key, Function Category, Status Bar Text,
    Help Context ID, Help File Name)*

  c Click . . . . | OK |

3 Click . . . . *desired command button*

Insert External Data into a Worksheet (Create a Query)

1 Select .... *cell where data will be inserted*

2 Click .... **Data, Get External Data...**
   NOTE: If Get External Data does not appear on the Data menu, see Install or Remove an Add-In, page 173.

   FROM SELECT DATA SOURCE DIALOG BOX

   ## To add a data source to the list:

   a Click .... | Other... |

   b Select a data source in .... **Enter Data Source** list
      NOTE: You click the New button to add one of the following data sources: Access Data, Btrieve Data, dBase Files, Excel Files, FoxPro Files, Oracle, Paradox, SQL Server or Text Files.

   c Click .... | OK |

3 Select desired data source in ..... **Available Data Sources** list

4 Click .... | Use |

5 Select file or table containing data to retrieve in ...... **Table** list

6 Click .... | Add |

7 Repeat step **3** and **4** for each file or table to add to query.

8 Click .... | Close |
   In the Query window, a field list appears in Table pane (upper pane) for each file or table you added. The field list contains the names of each field in the table.

9 Add (page 228) .... *fields to the Data pane*

10 Work with the result set in the data pane.
   (See topics in this section, pages 227-237.)

11 Click .... **File, Return Data to Microsoft Excel**

12 Select .... *Get External Data options:*
   Keep Query Definition, Include Field Names,
   Include Row Numbers, Destination

13 Click .... | OK |

Add Fields to the Data Pane

NOTE: The Data pane is the lower half of query window. When Automatic Query is off (page 229) and you add field(s), only the field name(s) will appear in the Data pane. Then, when you are ready to run the query, you can click the Query Now button (page 228) to show the data (the result set) in the Data pane columns.

FROM MICROSOFT QUERY
*(See **Insert External Data into a Worksheet**, page 227.)*

To add specific fields to Data pane:

1 Press **Ctrl** and click . . . . *each field to add in field list*

2 Drag . . . . *selection*
   onto . . . . *desired column position in Data pane*

To add all fields to Data pane in alphabetical order:

1 Double-click . . . . *title bar of field list*

2 Drag . . . . *any field in selected field list*
   onto . . . . *Data pane*

To add all fields to Data pane in order they were created:

• Double-click . . . . ** at top of field list*

Run Query when Automatic Query is Off

FROM MICROSOFT QUERY
*(See **Insert External Data into a Worksheet**, page 227.)*

• Click . . . . *Query Now button*

   NOTE: Automatic Query is on when the Auto Query button is recessed.

Turn Automatic Query On or Off

FROM MICROSOFT QUERY
(See Insert External Data into a Worksheet, page 227.)

- Click .... ***Auto Query button*** 🔁 or 🔁

    NOTE: *Automatic Query is on when the Auto Query button is recessed.*

Delete a Field Column in the Data Pane

FROM MICROSOFT QUERY
(See Insert External Data into a Worksheet, page 227.)

1 Click .... ***field name to delete***
2 Press .... Del

Move a Field Column in the Data Pane

FROM MICROSOFT QUERY
(See Insert External Data into a Worksheet, page 227.)

1 Click .... ***column heading to move***
2 Drag .... ***column***
  onto .... ***desired column position***
  Excel displays a dark column border where column will be inserted.

Size a Field Column in the Data Pane

FROM MICROSOFT QUERY
(See Insert External Data into a Worksheet, page 227.)

1 Point to .... ***right side of column heading to size***
2 Drag .... ***column border left or right***

Edit or Add Records in Result Set

WARNING: Changes made to records in the result set affect the data in the underlying data file or table.

NOTE: Microsoft Query may restrict the kind of data you can enter in a field based on the requirements of the underlying table. You can copy and move selected data in a record using the commands on the Edit menu.

FROM MICROSOFT QUERY
(See Insert External Data into a Worksheet, page 227.)

• Click . . . . **Records,** then select **Allow Editing**

To edit a record:

a Select . . . . *cell in record to edit*

b Edit . . . . *data as desired*

NOTE: A pencil graphic in the beginning of the row indicates the change has not yet been saved. Microsoft Query automatically saves the changes to the underlying file when you select another record, and you cannot undo the changes.

To add a record:

a Select . . . . *desired cell in last row of result set*
   The last row is marked with an asterisk (*).

b Type . . . . *data as desired*

To move to next or previous field in record:

• Press . . . . **Tab** or **Shift** + **Tab**

Delete Records in Result Set

WARNING: Changes made to records in the result set also changes the data in the underlying data file or table.

FROM MICROSOFT QUERY
*(See **Insert External Data into a Worksheet**, page 227.)*

1 Click .... **Records,** then select **Allow Editing**
2 Click .... *record selector of record to delete*
   NOTE: The record selector is the first unlabeled column in result set.

To delete a group of records:

- Press **Shift** and click ...... *last record selector in group*
3 Press .... `Del`
4 Click .... `OK`

Show or Hide Criteria Pane

FROM MICROSOFT QUERY
*(See **Insert External Data into a Worksheet**, page 227.)*

1 Click .... **View**
2 Select or deselect .... **Criteria**

Add Criteria (Filter Records Displayed in Result Set)

FROM MICROSOFT QUERY
*(See **Insert External Data into a Worksheet**, page 227.)*

1 Select .... *cell in result set*
containing criteria value.
NOTE: *The value can be of any data type. The value and the field
column it is in will be used as a starting point for the criteria you
will specify in the steps that follow.*

2 Click .... **Criteria, Add Criteria...**

To specify how to combine new criteria with a previous criteria:

- Select .... ◯ **And** or ◯ **Or**

3 If necessary, select field name in .... **Field:** [⬦]

4 Select an operator in .... **Operator:** [⬦]
that sets relationship of the field to the value(s).

5 Type value(s) in .... **Value:** [   ]
NOTE: *Separate multiple values with a comma.*

OR

a Click .... [**Values...**]

b Select value(s) in .... **Values** list

c Click .... [**OK**]

To set criteria for a totaled field:

- Select a function in .... **Total:** [   ]

6 Click .... [**Add**]

7 Click .... [**Close**]
Microsoft Query displays the criteria in a column in the Criteria pane.
NOTE: *When Automatic Query is off (page 229), you must run
the query (page 228) to see the changes in the result set.*

Set Properties of a Query

FROM MICROSOFT QUERY
(See Insert External Data into a Worksheet, page 227.)

1 Click . . . . **View, Query Properties...**

To show unique records only:

- Select . . . . ☐ **Unique Values Only**

To group records with identical values:

- Select . . . . ☐ **Group Records**

2 Click . . . . `OK`

Modify a Criteria

FROM MICROSOFT QUERY
(See Insert External Data into a Worksheet, page 227.)

1 If necessary, show (page 231) . . . . *Criteria pane*

2 Double-click . . . . *cell containing criteria element to change*

3 Select . . . . *Edit Criteria options:*
Operator, Value, Field, Total
NOTE: *Available options depend on part of criteria you double-clicked.*

4 Click . . . . `OK`
NOTE: *When Automatic Query is off (page 229), you must run
the query (page 228) to see the changes in the result set.*

Remove a Criteria

FROM MICROSOFT QUERY
(See Insert External Data into a Worksheet, page 227.)

1 If necessary, show (page 231) . . . . *Criteria pane*

2 Click . . . . *column selector above criteria to remove*
NOTE: *The column selector is the top narrow bar in the Criteria pane.*

3 Press . . . . `Del`
NOTE: *When Automatic Query is off (page 229), you must run
the query (page 228) to see the changes in the result set.*

Remove All Criteria

FROM MICROSOFT QUERY
*(See **Insert External Data into a Worksheet**, page 227.)*

• Click .... **Criteria, Remove All Criteria**
  NOTE: *When Automatic Query is off (page 229), you must run
  the query (page 228) to see the changes in the result set.*

Add Tables to Existing Query

FROM MICROSOFT QUERY
*(See **Insert External Data into a Worksheet**, page 227.)*

1 Click .... ***Add Table(s)*** 🔲

2 Select file or table containing data to retrieve in ...... **Table** list

3 Click .... [**Add**]

4 Repeat step **3** and **4** for each file or table to add to query.

5 Click .... [**Close**]
  *In the Query window, a field list appears in Table pane (upper pane)
  for each file or table you added. The field list contains the names of
  each field in the table.*

Delete a Table from Query

FROM MICROSOFT QUERY
*(See **Insert External Data into a Worksheet**, page 227.)*

1 Click .... ***field list of table to delete***

2 Press .... [Del]

Calculate a Field

Creates a new field based on the minimum value, maximum value, sum, average and count of values in a numeric field in the result set. If the field contains text, the available functions are count, minimum and maximum. The new field does not change the underlying file or table.

FROM MICROSOFT QUERY
(See Insert External Data into a Worksheet, page 227.)

1 Create . . . . **query that shows records to calculate**
   NOTE: *For example, add criteria so the result set shows only records for 1993 (DATE > #12/31/92# and DATE < #01/1/94#).*

2 Add only fields (page 228) . . . . **containing values to calculate**
   NOTE: *For example, add just the AMOUNT field if you want to calculate only values in the AMOUNT field; or add just the CATEGORY and AMOUNT fields if you want to find the total AMOUNT for each unique CATEGORY field in the result set.*

3 Select . . . . **any cell in field to calculate**

4 Click . . . . **Cycle thru Totals button** $\boxed{\Sigma}$
   until desired function appears in column heading.

   OR

   a Click . . . . **Records, Edit Column...**
   b Select a function in . . . . **Total:** $\boxed{}$
   c Click . . . . $\boxed{\text{OK}}$

NOTE: *When Automatic Query is off (page 229), you must run the query (page 228) to see the changes in the result set.*

Remove Calculated Field

FROM MICROSOFT QUERY
(See Insert External Data into a Worksheet, page 227.)

1 Select . . . . **any cell in field you have calculated**
2 Click . . . . **Records, Edit Column...**
3 Select blank item in . . . . **Total:** $\boxed{}$
4 Click . . . . $\boxed{\text{OK}}$

Join Tables

FROM MICROSOFT QUERY
*(See **Insert External Data into a Worksheet**, page 227.)*

1 If necessary, add (page 234) .... **tables to query**
you intend to join.
NOTE: *Microsoft Query may automatically join tables if they
contain the same primary key field.*

2 Click .... **Table, Joins**

3 Select name of table and field in .... **Left:** ⬚ ±
for which an equivalent field exists in table to join.
NOTE: *Each field name contains the name of the table
(lowercase letters), a period and the field name.*

4 Select operator in .... **Operator:** ⬚ ±

5 Select name of table and field in .... **Right:** ⬚ ±
to join with table selected in step **3**.
NOTE: *The field from this table should have the same field name
and contain the same type of data as the field selected in step **3**.*

6 Select .... **Join Includes option**
NOTE: *Available options will depend on the selections
made in steps **3-5**.*

7 Click .... [**Add**]

To remove a join:

a Select join to remove in .... **Joins in Query** list

b Click .... [**Remove**]

8 Click .... [**Close**]
Microsoft Query adds a join line indicating the key fields
in the joined tables.
NOTE: *You can quickly create a join by dragging the key field
from the field list in one table onto the key field in the table to
join. You can quickly remove a join by clicking its join line, and
pressing **Del**.*

Save the Query Design

FROM MICROSOFT QUERY
(See Insert External Data into a Worksheet, page 227.)

- Click .... *Save File button* 🖫

  If prompted,

  a Type name in .... **File Name:** [＿＿＿]

  b Click .... [OK]

Open a Saved Query Design

FROM MICROSOFT QUERY
(See Insert External Data into a Worksheet, page 227.)

1 Click .... *Open Query button* 📂

2 Select file in .... **File Name** list

3 Click .... [OK]

Close a Query

FROM MICROSOFT QUERY
(See Insert External Data into a Worksheet, page 227.)

1 Click .... **File, Close Query**

2 If prompted to save query, select from options provided.

Create Text Notes

1 Select . . . . *cell to attach note to*

2 Click . . . . **Insert, Note...**

3 Type note in . . . . **Text Note** box

To add notes to other cells:

a Click . . . . `Add`

b Select (in worksheet) or
type cell reference for note in . . . . **Cell:**

c Type note in . . . . **Text Note** box
NOTE: You can edit or delete existing text in Text Note box.

d Repeat steps **a-c**, as needed.

4 Click . . . . `OK`
Excel marks each cell containing a note with a note marker (small square).

View or Edit Text Notes

1 Select . . . . *cell containing note*
NOTE: Cells with notes have a small square in upper-right corner.

2 Click . . . . **Insert, Note...**

3 View or edit note in . . . . **Text Note** box

To view or edit additional notes:

a Select cell containing note in . . . . **Notes in Sheet** list

b View or edit note in . . . . **Text Note** box

c Repeat steps **a** and **b**, as needed.

4 Click . . . . `OK`

Attach a Sound File to a Note

NOTE: *Requires installation of a sound card and driver.*

1 Select .... *cell to attach note to*

2 Click .... Insert, No̲te...

3 Click .... `Import...`

4 Select .... *sound file*
*(See **Select Drive, Directory, or File(s)**, page 11.)*

5 Click .... `OK`
NOTE: *To attach a different sound file to a note, click OK then repeat this procedure from the beginning.*

To add the same sound note to other cells:

a Click .... `Add`

b Select (in worksheet) or
type cell reference for note in .... C̲ell:

c Repeat steps **a** and **b**, as needed.
Excel marks cells containing attached sound notes with an asterisk (*) in Notes in Sheet list.

6 Click .... `OK`
Excel marks cells containing notes with note markers (small squares).

Attach a Recorded Sound to a Note

NOTE: *Requires installation of a sound card and driver.*

1 Select .... *cell to attach note to*

2 Click .... Insert, No̲te...

3 Click .... `Record...`
NOTE: *The Record button is not available if cell already has a sound note attached to it.*

4 Click .... `●` Record

5 Record .... *note*
NOTE: *To pause the recording, click the Pause button.*

Continued ...

Attach a Recorded Sound to a Note (continued)

6 Click .... ■
Stop

   NOTE: To test the recording, click the Play button.

7 Click .... `OK`

   NOTE: To attach a different recording to a note, click OK then repeat this procedure from the beginning.

To add the same sound note to other cells:

a Click .... `Add`

b Select (in worksheet) or
type cell reference for note in .... **Cell:** ☐

c Repeat steps **a** and **b**, as needed.
Excel marks cells containing attached sound notes with an asterisk (*) in Notes in Sheet list.

8 Click .... `OK`

Play Back Sounds Attached to Notes

1 Select .... *cell containing note*

2 Click .... **Insert, Note...**

3 Click .... `Play`

To play back sounds attached to other notes:

a Select cell containing a sound in .... **Notes in Sheet** list
NOTE: Cells with attached sound have an asterisk (*).

b Click .... `Play`

c Repeat steps **a** and **b**, as needed.

4 Click .... `OK`

Erase Sounds Attached to Notes

Retains the text in a note that has both text and sound.

1 Select .... *cell containing note*

2 Click .... **Insert, Note...**

3 Click .... [Erase]
Excel changes the Erase button to Record after sound has been erased.

To erase sound notes attached to other cells:

a Select note containing sound in .... **Notes in Sheet** list
NOTE: Cells with attached sounds have an asterisk (*).

b Click .... [Erase]
NOTE: The asterisk (*) will remain until you exit the dialog box.

c Repeat steps **a** and **b**, as needed.

4 Click .... [OK]

Delete Notes

1 Select .... *cell(s) containing note(s)*

2 Click .... **Edit, Clear ►, Notes**

OR

1 Click .... **Insert, Note...**

2 Select note to delete in .... **Notes in Sheet** list

3 Click .... [Delete]

4 Click .... [OK]
to confirm deletion.

5 Repeat steps **2-4**, as needed.

6 Click .... [Close]

Use Info Window to View or Print Cell Details

1 Click .... **T**ools, **O**ptions...

2 Click .... [View]

3 Select .... ☐ Info **W**indow

4 Click .... [OK]

5 Click .... **W**indow, **A**rrange...

6 Select .... *Arrange option:*
Tiled, Horizontal, Vertical

7 Click .... [OK]

To add or remove information displayed:

a Select .... *Info window*

b Click .... **I**nfo
on menu bar.
NOTE: Check marks appear next to selected categories.

c Select or deselect .... *information category:*
*Cell, Formula, Value, Format, Protection,
Names, Precedents..., Dependents..., Note*

If Precedents or Dependents,

1. Select .... ○ **D**irect Only or ○ **A**ll Levels

2. Click .... [OK]

d Repeat steps **b** and **c** for each category to add or remove.

8 Select .... *cell in any worksheet*
to view its details.
*NOTE: To view cells containing specific contents in an Info window, refer to **Select Cells Containing Special Contents**, page 44.*

To print Info window information:

a Select .... *cells in worksheet*
containing information to print.

b Select .... *Info window*

c Click .... *Print button* 🖨

Close Info Window

- Double-click .... *Info window's control box* ⊟

Audit Worksheet

Excel's audit commands use arrows to trace precedents (cells referred to by formulas) and dependents (cells containing formulas that refer to the active cell). You can use these tools to debug your worksheet formulas. Tracer arrows are not saved with the workbook.

Show Auditing Toolbar

- Click ...... <u>T</u>ools, <u>A</u>uditing ▸, <u>S</u>how Auditing Toolbar

Trace Dependent Formulas

1 Select ...... *cell containing data referred to by a formula*

2 Click .... *Trace Dependents button*
on Auditing toolbar (*see above*).
NOTE: *If Tracer arrows do not appear, see **Set View Options**, page 173, and deselect the Hide All option.*

Remove Dependent Tracer Arrows

1 Select .... *cell containing data used by a formula*

2 Click .... *Remove Dependent Arrows button*
on Auditing toolbar (*see above*).

Trace Precedent Data and Formulas

1 Select .... *cell containing formula*

2 Click . ... *Trace Precedents button*
on Auditing toolbar (*see above*).
NOTE: *If Tracer arrows do not appear, see **Set View Options**, page 173, and deselect the Hide All option*

Remove Precedent Tracer Arrows

1 Select . . . . *cell containing formula*

2 Click . . . . *Remove Precedent Arrows button*
on Auditing toolbar (*page 243*).

Remove All Tracer Arrows

• Click . . . . *Remove All Arrows button*
on Auditing toolbar (*page 243*).

Select Cell at End of Tracer Arrows

1 Double-click . . . . *tracer arrow*

2 Repeat step **1** to select cell at opposite end.

Trace Possible Error Source in a Formula

1 Click . . . . *cell containing error value*

2 Click . . . . *Trace Error button*
on Auditing toolbar (*page 243*).

About Cells

Cells are areas in a worksheet or macro sheet in which data is stored. Each cell is defined by the intersection of a row and column (such as A3, denoting column A, row 3). A **cell reference** identifies a cell or a range of cells.

About Formulas

Formulas are mathematical expressions that create new values by combining numerical values with operators (plus, minus, etc.). Formulas may contain cell references, (relative, absolute or mixed), operators, and functions. See the topics that follow.

Relative Cell References

A **relative cell reference** (such as A2) describes a cell's location based on its relationship to another cell.

Formula example: =**A2***10

This formula multiplies the contents of cell A2 by 10. The cell reference A2 will change to B2 if you copy this formula one cell position to the right. The copied formula will become =**B2***10.

Absolute Cell References

An **absolute cell reference** (such as $A$2) describes an exact cell location. Use a dollar sign ($) before both the column letter and the row number to specify an absolute cell reference.

Formula example: =**$A$2***10

This formula multiplies the contents of cell A2 by 10. The cell reference $A$2 will not change if you copy the formula to another cell. The copied formula would remain =**$A$2***10

Mixed Cell References

A **mixed cell reference** (such as $A2) describes a cell location with relative and absolute parts. The dollar sign ($) marks the absolute part of the reference while the unmarked part (2) defines the relative part of the reference.

Formula example: =**$A2***10

This formula multiplies the contents of cell A2 by 10. Only the relative part of the cell reference will adjust if you copy the formula one cell position to the right. The copied formula would become =**$A3***10.

Cell References (Examples)

The tables that follow show examples of how to use reference operators to cell references you might use in formulas. You can also use named references with these operators.

References to cells in the <u>same worksheet</u>

Colons (:) between references indicate a range of cells between and including the two references.

Commas (,) between references indicate a union (one reference that includes the two references) of the cells.

A **space** between references indicate a single cell location where the two references intersect.

To refer to:	Reference examples
a **range** of cells (adjacent cells)	C5:E5
a **union** of non-adjacent cells	C5,E5
an **intersection** of two ranges	C5:C10 A7:E7
all of **column C**	C:C
all of **row 3**	3:3
all of **rows 3 through 5**	3:5
the **entire worksheet**	A:IV *or* 1:16384
a **named reference**, "sales"	sales

References to cells in <u>another worksheet</u>

Exclamation signs (!) separate the sheet name from the cell reference

Colons (:) between worksheet names indicate a range of worksheets
Use **quotation marks** if worksheet name contains a space.

To refer to:	Reference examples
cells in a **different worksheet** (Sales 93)	"Sales 93"!A1:D1
a **3-D reference** to cells in range of worksheets (Ranges A1:D4 on sheets Sheet3 through Sheet5)	Sheet3:Sheet5!A1:D4

References to cells in <u>another workbook</u> (External References or Links)

Single quotations (') enclose the path, filename and sheet-level name when creating a sheet-level reference.

Square brackets ([ ]) enclose the workbook filename.

Exclamation signs (!) separate the sheet name from the cell reference.

To refer to:	Reference examples
cells in a **different workbook** (sheet-level)	'c:\excel\[sales.xls]sheet2'!D1:D10
named cells in a **different workbook** (book-level).	'c:\excel\[sales.xls]'!sales

Arithmetic Operators

Arithmetic operators direct Excel to carry out mathematical operations The following is a list of arithmetic operators that can be used in formulas:

+	Addition	*	Multiplication
-	Subtraction	/	Division
%	Percentage of	^	Exponentiation

Formula example: =2*(A1+B4)

This formula calculates and displays the sum of values contained in cells A1 and B4, multiplied by 2.

Comparison Operators

Comparison operators compare values and produce the logical value TRUE or FALSE. The following is a list of comparison operators that can be used in formulas:

=	Equal
>=	Greater than or equal to
>	Greater than
<=	Less than or equal to
<	Less than
<>	Not equal to

Formula example: =IF(A1=B2,"equal","unequal")

This formula compares values contained in cells A1 and B2, then displays equal if it is true (that A1 equals B2); if not, it displays unequal.

Text Operator

A text operator combines text values into one value. Use an ampersand (&) to combine text values.

Formula example: =A1&B10

This formula combines and displays text contained in cells A1 and B10. If cell A1 contains MICRO, and B10 contains SOFT, the result of this formula would be MICROSOFT.

About Worksheet Functions

Worksheet functions are prewritten formulas that can be used alone or as part of a formula. Use the Paste function command from the Formula menu to list the many functions Excel provides.
The following are some examples of worksheet functions to be used with Excel:

> **AVERAGE**(number1,number2,...)
>
> **NPV**(rate,value1,value2,...)
>
> **SUM**(number1,number2,...)

Formula example: =AVERAGE(A1:B10)

This formula calculates and displays the mean average of values contained in the cell range A1:B10.

NOTE: *The* **Function Wizard** *helps you to build and understand functions It lets you select functions from the following categories*

Most Recently Used	*All*
Financial	*Date & Time*
Math and Trig	*Statistical*
Lookup & Reference	*Database*
Text	*Logical*
Information	

Using Functions to Evaluate Conditions

The **IF** function and the **AND**, **OR**, and **NOT** logical functions are useful for evaluating cell contents and can be used together to evaluate complex conditions:

IF(condition,true,false)   **OR(condition)**

NOT(condition)   **AND(condition)**

In the examples that follow, the cell containing the value 90 has been named **Temp** and the cell containing the value 70 has been named **Hum**. In the first sample function below, the IF function returns the first value ("HOT") because the condition (Temp >=90) is <u>true</u>.

Temp	Hum
90	70

Sample functions:	*Return:*
=IF(<u>Temp>=90</u>,"<u>HOT</u>","NOT HOT")	*HOT*
=NOT(Temp=67)	*FALSE*
=IF(AND(Temp>=90,Hum>=70),"SULTRY","OK")	*SULTRY*
=IF(OR(Temp>=90,Hum>=80),"STICKY","OK")	*STICKY*
=IF(NOT(Temp=90),"IT IS NOT 90","IT'S 90")	*IT'S 90*

Checking for Numbers in Cells

The **ISNUMBER** function is useful for checking to see if the contents of a cell is a number. You can use this function with the IF function to perform a calculation only if a cell contains a number. In the example that follows, the ISNUMBER function checks to see if cell B3 contains a number. If B3 contains a number (evaluates to **true**), the IF function multiplies B3 by 10 (**B3*10**). If B3 is not a number, the IF function returns the character value "Not a Number."

Sample function:

=IF(ISNUMBER(B3),**B3*10**,"Not a Number")

If the contents of B3 is 10, returns 100
If the contents of B3 is not a number, returns "Not a Number"

Using the AND Function to Evaluate Two Conditions

The **AND** function is useful for checking two conditions. For example, you can use the AND function with the IF function to perform a calculation only if *both* cells contains a number. In the example that follows, the ISNUMBER function checks to see if cell B2 *and* cell B3 contain a number. If both contain numbers (evaluate to *true*), the IF function multiplies B2 by B3. If either cell does not contain a number, the IF function returns the character value "Not Numbers."

NOTE: *When combining (nesting) functions like this, be careful to include the required parentheses. It's easy to leave one out!*

Sample function:

`IF(AND(ISNUMBER(B2),ISNUMBER(B3)),B2*B3,"Not Numbers")`

If B2 is 10 and B3 is 20, returns 200
If B2 and B3 are not numbers, returns "Not Numbers"

NOTE: *You can use the OR function instead of the AND function if either (not both) conditions must be true before the IF function carries out the specified action*

252

Appendix

How Excel Adjusts References

When you create formulas that reference cells, and then make changes to the worksheet (like moving cells or inserting rows or columns), Excel will often adjust the references relative to the number of cells involved in the action.

Action:	Reference adjustment:
Move cells	Absolute and relative references adjust.
Copy cells	Relative references adjust. Absolute references are retained.
Insert/delete cells	All reference types adjust.
Insert/delete sheets within a 3-D reference*	3-D reference adjusts. For example, if you delete a sheet within a 3-D reference, the 3-D reference will reference remaining sheets in the reference.
Move sheets at either end of a 3-D reference*	3-D reference adjusts. For example, if you move a sheet that ends a reference, six positions to the right, the 3-D reference will reference all sheets between the two sheets.

** 3-D references are indicated by a starting and ending sheet name. Here is an example of a 3-D reference in a formula: =SUM(Sheet1:Sheet4!A1:D5). The 3-D reference includes the range of cells A1:D5 in the worksheets **Sheet1** through **Sheet4**.*

ERROR MESSAGES: If an error message occurs after you change a worksheet, refer to Formula Error Messages and Possible Causes, on the following page.

Formula Error Messages and Possible Causes

Below is a list of error values that may appear in cells when Excel cannot calculate the formula for that cell.

#DIV/0!   Indicates that the formula is trying to divide by zero

In formula: • Divisor is a zero. • Divisor is referencing a blank cell or a cell that contains a zero value

#N/A   Indicates that no value is available.

In formula • An invalid argument may have been used with a LOOKUP function. • A reference in an array formula does not match range in which results are displayed. • A required argument has been omitted from a function.

#NAME?   Indicates that Excel does not recognize the name used in a formula.

In formula: • A named reference has been deleted or has not been defined. • A function or name reference has been misspelled. • Text has been entered without required quotation marks. • A colon has been omitted in a range reference.

#NULL!   Indicates that the intersection of two range references does not exist.

In formula: • Two range references (separated with a space operator) have been used to represent a non-existent intersection of the two ranges.

#NUM!   Indicates a number error.

In formula: • An incorrect value has been used in a function. • Arguments result in a number too small or large to be represented.

Continued ...

Formula Error Messages and Possible Causes (continued)

#REF!   Indicates reference to an invalid cell.

In formula: • Arguments refer to cells that have been deleted or overwritten with non-numeric data. The argument is replaced with #REF!

#VALUE!   Indicates the invalid use of an operator or argument

In formula: • An invalid value or a referenced value has been used with a formula or function (i.e , SUM("John"))

Circular   A message that indicates formula is referencing itself.

In formula: • A cell reference refers to the cell containing the formula result.

*NOTE: If a circular reference is intended, you can select the **Iteration** option (page 88). Iteration is an instruction to repeat a calculation until a specific result value is met.*

In most cases, the noun is the primary index key.
For example, look up "Sheets, select" instead of "Select, sheets."

In most cases, the noun is the primary index key.
For example, look up "Sheets, select" instead of "Select, sheets."

In most cases, the noun is the primary index key.
For example, look up "Sheets, select" instead of "Select, sheets."

In most cases, the noun is the primary index key.
For example, look up "Sheets, select" instead of "Select, sheets."

In most cases, the noun is the primary index key.
For example, look up "Sheets, select" instead of "Select, sheets."

260

Index

In most cases, the noun is the primary index key.
For example, look up "Sheets, select" instead of "Select, sheets."

In most cases, the noun is the primary index key.
For example, look up "Sheets, select" instead of "Select, sheets."

262

Index

*In most cases, the noun is the primary index key.
For example, look up "Sheets, select" instead of "Select, sheets."*

In most cases, the noun is the primary index key.
For example, look up "Sheets, select" instead of "Select, sheets."

In most cases, the noun is the primary index key.
For example, look up "Sheets, select" instead of "Select, sheets."

In most cases, the noun is the primary index key.
For example, look up "Sheets, select" instead of "Select, sheets."

In most cases, the noun is the primary index key.
For example, look up "Sheets, select" instead of "Select, sheets."

In most cases, the noun is the primary index key.
For example, look up "Sheets, select" instead of "Select, sheets."

In most cases, the noun is the primary index key.
For example, look up "Sheets, select" instead of "Select, sheets."

In most cases, the noun is the primary index key.
For example, look up "Sheets, select" instead of "Select, sheets."

In most cases, the noun is the primary index key.
For example, look up "Sheets, select" instead of "Select, sheets."

In most cases, the noun is the primary index key.
For example, look up "Sheets, select" instead of "Select, sheets."

In most cases, the noun is the primary index key.
For example, look up "Sheets, select" instead of "Select, sheets."

More Quick Reference Guides